Foundation Care

TRAINEE HANDBOOK

For the **TOPSS** *Standards*

Yvonne Nolan

Heinemann Educational Publishers, Halley Court,
Jordan Hill, Oxford OX2 8EJ

Part of Harcourt Education Limited

Heinemann is the registered trademark of Harcourt Education Limited

First published 2002

06 05 04 03 02
10 9 8 7 6 5 4 3 2 1

0 435 40131 9

Typeset by TechType, Abingdon, Oxon
Printed in UK by The Bath Press

Acknowledgements
This book has benefited from the major contribution to Unit 3 by Val
Michie, whose support was invaluable in completing the work. As
always Mary James at Heinemann kept faith, and family, friends and
colleagues have made this work possible despite the challenges.

The authors and publishers would like to thank the following for
permission to reproduce photographs: Alamy, pages 13, 20, 45, 70 and
76; John Birdsall, page 33; Corbis, pages 57 and 106; S & R Greenhill,
page 53; Harcourt Education/Gerald Sunderland, page 102.

Cover: Nonstock/Image State

Dedication
This book is dedicated to all those who give and receive care.

Contents

Introduction

Welcome to work in care and welcome to this book. You may be using the book because you have recently begun to work in the care sector, or have recently moved jobs. In either case, you will be extending and developing your skills and experience.

Working in care is like few other jobs. The greatest influence on the way someone feels about the care they receive is you – only a few other careers rely so heavily on the attitudes, values and communication skills of the people providing the service. Think about it: someone could be cared for in the smartest surroundings, which would be very pleasant, but he or she would not have a good experience if the people providing the care were offhand, prejudiced or downright uncaring! The way you prepare yourself for your work will have a direct effect on the service users who receive your services throughout your career.

The foundations of good practice and sound values which you develop at this early stage will provide a firm basis for all your work regardless of how far you progress, and whatever your ultimate responsibilities. The book is designed to support you and to provide you with opportunities to look at your own practice, but also to raise questions and issues you can discuss with your own manager or supervisor.

Using the book

During your first six months in your new job, you will need to produce evidence to show that you have begun to understand the main aspects of the care sector. The units of this book relate directly to each of the five Foundation Standards:

1 Understand how to apply the value base of care
2 Communicate effectively
3 Develop as a worker
4 Recognise and respond to abuse and neglect
5 Understand the experiences and particular needs of the individuals using the service.

Each unit will look in detail at the information you need to help you to think about this area of your work. It will also give you some ideas for further questions to ask and some exercises which will help you to think about the issues – you will probably be surprised at how much you already know! Your manager or supervisor may have developed a programme of training and development in which you will have the opportunity to learn about all the areas of care practice in the Foundation Standards. The training will be designed to help you to look at how you apply everything you have learned in your own workplace – learning always makes more sense if you can see how you will use it in practice. Your manager or supervisor may use the support materials from the Resource Pack designed to go with this book. If so, you will find that many of the ideas, information and exercises relate to the materials you are using in your training programme, and that some of the exercises in this book will help to provide the evidence your manager or supervisor will need to show that you have understood the Foundation Standards.

Induction and Foundation

In your first six weeks in your job, you will have participated in an induction programme, based on the Induction Standards. The purpose of the induction programme is to make sure that you understand the process and procedures of the organisation you are working for, and also that you can work safely in your work setting. The induction programme will form the basis for your continuing training and development using the Foundation Standards. The two sets of standards are linked, and you will find that the Foundation Standards build on the Induction Standards. There is a table on pages 111–113 which shows how each standard is linked to the others. You may find this useful if you want to follow up some of the learning or information from your induction.

Neither set of standards is intended to be a training course, nor is it any kind of hurdle or barrier you have to cross – there are no tests or exams. Both sets of standards are, however, intended to show you and your manager the areas of practice about which you need to have some understanding. The amount of knowledge and understanding you need will be different depending on where you work and the kind of job you do. Your manager will have decided which aspects of the standards are particularly important for your work and which are less relevant. You will work your way through the standards in line with the plan your own manager has developed.

I hope you find the book useful as a reference point and in providing you with some food for thought. The support you need during this early time in your job role will come, above all, from your manager or supervisor. However, the motivation to continue to develop your own knowledge and skills will come from the service users you work with. They are the ones who will benefit from your increasing experience and ability.

Making sure that you have the understanding identified in these standards is a sound basis for your future career. I wish you every success in becoming the best practitioner you can be.

Foundation standard 1
Understand how to apply the value base of care

In order to work effectively, you need to know about the practical ways in which your work follows the values of the care sector. Everyone who works in this sector is guided by its **value base**. This is a set of principles which underpin the way you work in any part of the care sector. These principles are important because they mean that anyone who receives care of any type should be treated in a fair and acceptable way, regardless of where and how they receive the service. If there was no accepted value base, then people could be treated differently if they were receiving care in hospital, in residential care or in the community, and this would lead to confusion and uncertainty about the quality of services.

Knowing why the value base is important is an essential step in understanding how to use it when you are doing your job. It is the basis you will need for all the work you do throughout your career in care.

What you are going to learn about:

- how to promote the empowerment of service users
- how to promote achievement and fulfilment
- how to recognise and work with constraints and conflicts
- how to promote anti-discriminatory practice.

1.1
Promote the empowerment of service users

What is empowerment and why is it important?

Empowerment is about making sure that people are able to make choices, and that they can take as much control of their lives as possible. Helping people make choices is a vital part of providing care as a service. Promoting empowerment simply means doing everything you can in your own practice and in your own work setting to make sure that this happens.

Many people who receive care services are often unable to make a lot of choices about their lives. This can be because of a range of different circumstances, but it can be because of the way essential services are provided. In our own daily lives we take many things for granted – you can usually make basic choices in your life without even having to think about them. For example:

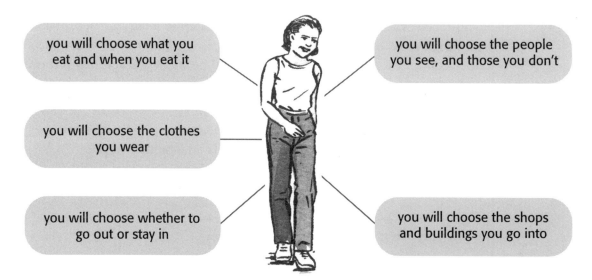

you will choose what you eat and when you eat it

you will choose the people you see, and those you don't

you will choose the clothes you wear

you will choose whether to go out or stay in

you will choose the shops and buildings you go into

Most of the time you give little thought to these choices. However, if you consider the service users in your own setting, you will realise that not all of them have the same options and choices as you do.

Try it out

For a couple of days, keep a list of the choices you make about everyday aspects of your life – use some of the examples above to start you off, but you will soon notice many more.

Now, think about the service users in your work setting. Write down next to each item on your list the names of service users who are also able to make the same choice. Do these service users have all of the same choices as you?

People who cannot make many choices can begin to feel that they are powerless in relation to their day-to-day activities. How much we value ourselves – our **self-esteem** – is a result of many factors, but a very important one is:

* the extent of control, or power, we have over our lives.

Of course, many other factors influence our self-esteem, such as:

* the amount of encouragement and praise we have had from important people in our lives, like parents and teachers
* whether we have positive and happy relationships with other people
* the amount of stimulation and satisfaction we get from our work – paid or unpaid.

Service users who are unable to exercise choice and control may very soon have lower self-esteem and lose confidence in their own abilities. Unfortunately, this means they may become convinced that they are unable to do many tasks for themselves, and that they need help in most areas of their day-to-day life. It is easy to see how such a chain of events can result in people becoming dependent on others and less able to do things for themselves. Once this downward spiral has begun it can be difficult to stop, so it is far better to avoid the factors which can make it begin.

Service users should be able to make choices

Self-esteem has a major effect on people's health and well-being. People with a confident, positive view of themselves, who believe that they have value and worth, are far more likely to be happy and healthy than those whose self-esteem is poor and whose confidence is low.

There is no doubt that emotional and psychological factors have a great influence on the progress and development of illness and disease. This is partly because of the effect of a positive outlook on lifestyle and behaviour. People who have a positive and confident outlook are far more likely to be interested and active in the world around them, while those lacking confidence and belief in their own abilities are more likely to be withdrawn and reluctant to try anything new. It is easy to see how this can affect a person's quality of life and reduce his or her overall health and well-being.

Check your learning

Make notes about the differences which could be made to the life of each service user you work with if he or she were able to make more choices. Use the list you made for the activity on page 2.

Note down what you think the effect could be for each person.

Empowerment for service users

Empowerment means that people can make choices about the services they receive and the ways in which they receive them. For example, it is often the case that service users are told the level of support they will receive and the days on which they will receive it. They may even be told the times at which they will receive such help. The reasons for this are obvious: all services have limited budget and staff resources, and these have to be managed in order to provide the best possible service for the largest number of people. However, this leaves a circle to be squared. Organisations who plan and deliver services have to respond on a general scale; they will try to take into account individual needs, but the nature of organisations makes it difficult to do so effectively. The point at which practices can be adapted to meet needs and empower individual service users, their families and carers, is when the care worker delivering the service meets and interacts with the service user. There are many ways in which you can ensure that your own practice empowers service users as far as possible.

> **Empowerment means:**
>
> ✓ making sure that people are able to make choices as much as possible
> ✓ promoting people's self-esteem and confidence
> ✓ helping people to take action for themselves where appropriate.

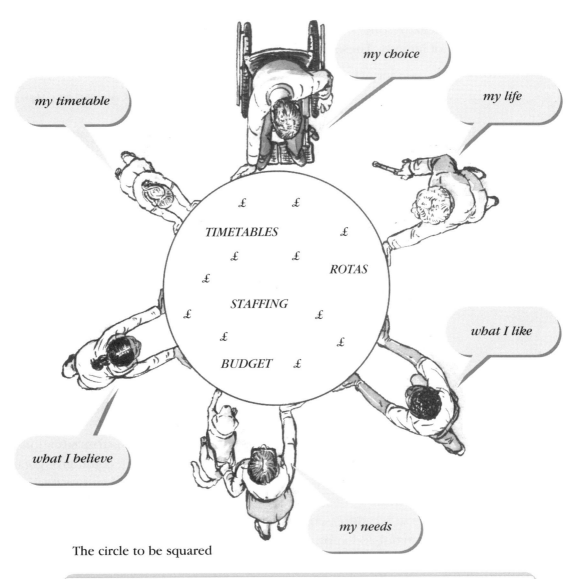

The circle to be squared

Ways you can promote empowerment

Promoting empowerment is about identifying the practical steps you can take in day-to-day working activities to give service users more choice and more opportunities to take decisions about their own lives. Much of this will depend on your work setting and the particular needs of the service users you care for. There are, however, some aspects of empowerment which are common to many settings and most service users, and these are the ones we discuss in the following pages.

If self-esteem is about ways we *value* ourselves, **self-concept** (or self-image) is about ways we *see* ourselves. These two are different, but both are equally important. Self-concept is about what makes people who they are, and makes them different from one another. Everyone has a concept of themselves – it can be a positive image overall or a negative one, but a great many factors contribute to an individual sense of identity. These will include:

- gender: whether a person is male or female
- race: whether a person is white, Asian or Black African in origin
- the language and accent a person uses
- the values and beliefs a person holds – for example, about which foods or ways of dressing are appropriate
- a person's religion
- sexual orientation: a person could be gay or lesbian.

All of these are aspects of our lives which contribute towards our idea of who we are.

As a care worker it is essential that you consider each of the service users you work with as an individual. As part of empowering service users, you will need to consider how you can promote their own sense of identity. This is not as difficult as it sounds! It is about making sure that you recognise that the values, beliefs, tastes and preferences which service users have – the things that make them who they are – must be supported, nurtured and encouraged, and not ignored and discounted because they are inconvenient or don't fit in with the care system.

In your role as a care worker, you will often come across situations where a little thought or a small change in practice could give greater opportunities for people to feel that they are valued and respected as individuals. For example, you may need to find out how a service user likes to be addressed. Do they consider that 'Mr' or 'Mrs' is more respectful and appropriate, or are they happy for a first name to be used? This, particularly for some older people, can be an important way of indicating respect.

You will need to give thought to the values and beliefs which service users may have, for example:

- religious or cultural beliefs about eating specific foods
- values about forms of dress which are acceptable
- beliefs or preferences about who should be able to provide personal care.

What you need to do

You need to make sure that people have been asked about religious or cultural preferences and those preferences are recorded so that all care workers and others providing care are able to access them.

There may already be arrangements in your workplace to ask for and record this information. If so, you must ensure that you are familiar with the process and that you know where to find the information for every service user you work with. If your workplace does not have arrangements in place to find out about people's choices and preferences, you should discuss with your line manager ways in which you can help to find this out.

How you need to do it

The prospect of having to ask people questions about their background, values and beliefs can be quite daunting. But it is quite rare for people to be offended by your showing an interest in them! Simple, open questions, asked politely, are always the best way.

Excuse me Mr Khan, the information I have here notes that you are a Muslim. Can you tell me about any particular foods you do not wish to eat?

You can obtain some information by observation – for instance looking at someone can tell you a lot about his or her preferences in dress. Particular forms of clothing worn for religious or cultural reasons are usually obvious (a turban or a sari, for instance, are easy to spot), but other forms of dress may also give you some clues about the person wearing them. Think about how dress can tell you about the amount of money people are used to spending on clothes or what kind of background they come from. Clothes also tell you a lot about someone's age and the type of lifestyle they are likely to be used to. Beware, however – any information you think you gain from this type of observation must be confirmed by checking your facts. Otherwise it is easy to be caught out – some people from wealthy backgrounds wear cheap clothes, and some people in their seventies wear the latest fashions and have face lifts!

Try it out

Look at the form, or other means of recording information, which is used in your workplace to set down the cultural or religious preferences of service users. Fill it in as if you were a service user. Note down all the factors which make you who you are. Think about:

- gender
- age
- background
- economic and social circumstances
- nationality
- religion
- sexual orientation
- food preferences
- entertainment preferences
- relaxation preferences
- reading material preferences.

Look back at the form you completed – would it tell a care worker enough about you, so they could ensure you were able to be the same person you were before receiving a care service? If not, think about which other questions you would need to be asked and note them down. Make sure that, if appropriate, you ask these questions of your service users.

How to give people choice

In the activity on page 2 you looked at the limitations experienced by some people in making choices about their lives. One of the major ways in which you can promote empowerment is to support service users in being able to make choices. This could be something relatively simple like asking 'what time would you like to eat?', although even this may not be easy to achieve in some residential settings. It could be something far more complex, like making difficult travel and mobility arrangements for someone to get to a particular place for a religious service or a family or social occasion.

Where service users want to make choices about their lives, you should ensure that you do your best to help them to identify any barriers they meet and then offer support in overcoming them. If you are working with service users who are living in their own homes, it is likely to be easier for them to make day-to-day choices about their lives. In some situations they may require help and support in order to achieve their choice, but it is generally less restrictive than a residential or hospital setting, where the needs of many other people also have to be taken into account.

For many disabled service users living in their own homes, the direct payment scheme has provided a far higher level of choice and empowerment than was possible previously. This system means that payments covering the provision of services are made directly to the disabled service user, who then employs carers directly and determines his or her own levels and types of service. If you think about the implications of this and how it changes the relationship between the disabled service user and the care workers, you can see clearly how this system puts the disabled service user in a position of power – the exact opposite of the position of many other service users, who are not able to exercise that level of control over the services they receive.

You will not be in a position to offer service users a great deal of choice over the types of services they receive, but you can certainly take steps to ensure that, as far as possible, they are able to make choices about important aspects of their lives. Here are some simple steps to follow.

Empowerment: allowing people to make choices

1. Always ask service users if this is the service they want and if this is the way they want to receive it.
2. Ask if they want other alternatives, either in the service or in the way it is delivered.
3. Look for ways you can support service users in achieving the choice they want – not for reasons why this is impossible!

The process doesn't have to turn into one where you ask a series of demanding questions. It can simply be a matter of checking with the service user as you work, as in the example on the next page.

Mrs Jones, would you like to wear the blue dress today, or is there another one you would prefer?

Well, I did want to wear that grey spotty skirt with the pink blouse today, but I don't think it's back from the laundry, so I can't.

Let me go down to the laundry and find out if it's ready. If there's any way I can get it for you, I will.

Thank you

The worker in this example has offered Mrs Jones a choice about clothes. Mrs Jones has indicated that she is not happy with the choice offered, and she has also identified the possible barrier to having the clothes she wants. The care worker has looked for a way that the barrier may possibly be overcome. This process can be used in a wide range of situations.

Sometimes service users are not able, because of the nature of a particular condition or illness, to identify choices or to participate in decision making. In these circumstances, it is important that you make every effort to involve them as far as they are able. For example, if a service user communicates differently from you as the result of a particular condition, or there are language differences, then it is important that you ensure that the communication differences are reduced as far as possible so that the service user can take part in discussions and decisions. This may involve using specific communication techniques, or arranging to have help from an appropriate specialist, for example:

- if you are communicating with a deaf service user, you may need to arrange for a sign language interpreter
- if you are communicating with someone who has speech difficulties following a stroke, you may need to use gestures or signs
- if you are communicating with a service user whose first language you do not speak, you will need to use an interpreter.

All of these steps will allow service users to be involved in decisions.

In other circumstances, you may be dealing with service users who are not able to fully participate in decisions about their day-to-day lives because they have a different level of understanding. This could, for example, include service users with learning difficulties, dementia or brain injury. In this situation, it may be that the service user has an advocate who represents his or her interests and is able to present a point of view to those who are providing services. The advocate may be a professional such as a solicitor, social worker or rights worker, or it could be a relative or friend. It is essential that you include the advocate in discussions as far as possible, to make sure that the service user's point of view is taken into account.

The importance of respect

Treating service users with dignity and respect is an essential aspect of empowerment. Self-esteem is about how people value themselves, and they cannot value themselves if they don't feel valued by others.

Recognising the unique and valuable aspects of each individual is an important part of being a successful care worker. Even if some of the service users you work with seem to have very different attitudes and approaches to life than you, or if they seem to have little understanding of their surroundings, they are still individuals with a history and with special and particular contributions to offer. Making sure that someone feels valued is not difficult; it is simply a matter of acknowledging what people do and the things they say, and showing that their actions and comments are appreciated. Saying 'Thank you, Mrs Thomas, that has been really helpful' after a discussion about service delivery may be all that is needed for the service user to feel that her views have been appreciated and taken into account.

It is also important to remember that each individual had a life before you knew them – it is easy to forget that most service users once didn't need care workers! The poem set out below will make you think. It is said to have been found in a hospital locker after the death of an elderly long-stay patient called Kate.

> What do you see, nurses, what do you see?
> What are you thinking when you look at me?
> A crabbit old woman, not very wise,
> Uncertain of habit with far-away eyes
> Who dribbles her food and makes no reply
> When you say in a loud voice 'I do wish you'd try'.
> Who seems not to notice the things that you do
> And forever is losing a stick or a shoe
> Who unresistingly or not lets you do as you will,
> With bathing and feeding – the long day to fill.
> Is that what you're thinking? Is that what you see?
> Then open your eyes nurse – you're looking at me.
> I'll tell you who I am as I sit here so still
> As I move at your bidding, as I eat at your will.
>
> I'm a small child of ten with a father and mother,
> Brothers and sisters who love one another.
> A young girl of sixteen with wings on her feet,
> Dreaming that soon a lover she'll meet.
> A bride soon, at twenty my heart gives a leap
> Remembering the vows that I promised to keep.
> At twenty-five now I have young of my own
> Who need me to build a secure happy home.
> A young woman of thirty, my young now grow fast
> Bound to each other with ties that should last.
> At forty my young ones now grown will be gone
> But my memory stays beside me to see I don't mourn.
> At fifty, once more babies play round my knee
> Again, we know children, my loved one and me.
> Dark days are upon me: my husband is dead
> I look at the future, I shudder with dread,
> For my young are all busy rearing young of their own
> And I think of the years and the love I have known.
> I'm an old woman now and nature is cruel

The body it crumbles, grace and vigour depart
There now is a stone where I once had a heart.
But inside this old carcass a young girl still dwells
And now and again my battered heart swells
I remember the joys, I remember the pain
And I'm loving and living life over again
I think of the years – all too few – gone too fast
And accept the stark fact that nothing can last.
So open your eyes, nurses, open and see
Not a crabbit old woman … look closer, see ME.

It's easy to forget that service users have a life history of their own

Check your learning

1. Describe how Kate feels about her treatment by her nurses.
2. What do Kate's nurses fail to see when they look at her?

It is very easy to make the service users you work with feel they are not valued, like Kate did. All it takes is a failure to consider people as important individuals who have a valuable contribution to make. If this poem makes an impact on you, remember it and think back to the feelings contained in it. Keep checking that your practice could never make anyone feel like the writer did.

Families and carers

Most service users have families and other people who care for them. They are an essential part of their lives and provide key support, both physically and emotionally. Valuing individuals and empowering them also means recognising the significance of those who support and care for the service user. Their role is vital, and, as long as the service user wishes, they should be involved in planning and discussing the level and type of service which will be delivered. As a professional carer, your role is clearly different from that of a family carer, but it is not better or superior – just different. Many carers are intimidated by the attitude of care workers, who can make them feel that they lack the level of skills which professional carers have. This may be the case, but they have the trust and confidence of the service user, and in many cases their experience of providing practical care for him or her is more valuable than all the technical skill of a professional. Making arrangements for carers and supporters to be a part of the process of care provision is a vital part of your role in empowering the service user.

You can do this in several ways – always remembering to check with the service user that this is what he or she wants:

- include carers and families in planning meetings
- include carers and families in review meetings
- make sure you speak to carers and families on a regular basis as part of monitoring the service provided
- always make a point of recognising and acknowledging the care being provided by the family or carer
- make sure that families and carers know how and when they can contact you.

Activity 1.1.1 and 1.1.2 Empowerment

Write down in your own words what empowerment means. Now test your understanding by answering the questions following the scenario below. Even if you work with a different service user group, this situation is likely to be relevant.

E is 78 years old, and she lives alone in her own home. She is mentally alert, but is profoundly deaf. E has difficulty in undertaking day-to-day domestic tasks and some of her personal care as she has severe osteoporosis which has made movement difficult and painful. Presently E receives care three times a week, offering support with domestic activities and bathing. It is proposed that the timing of her visits will be altered, so that the carer will visit in the afternoon instead of the morning as at present.

1. How will you ensure that E is made aware of the proposed change?
2. What steps will you take to allow her to express her views about the change?
3. How will you make sure that E's views are treated with respect?
4. How will you make sure that E feels valued during the process?
5. How can you empower E in this situation?
6. Why is it important to empower service users?

If appropriate, think about the ways the issues would differ for the service user group you work with.

1.2
Promote achievement and fulfilment

The feeling of having achieved something is a feeling everyone can identify with – regardless of the size of the achievement or its significance when viewed from a wider perspective. Most achievements which give us pleasure are relatively small – passing a driving test, finishing a run, clearing a garden, passing an exam, putting together a set of flat-pack bookshelves ... Achievement does not have to mean reaching the North Pole, or climbing Everest, or winning the World Cup. Achievements that are much smaller and closer to home are those which provide a sense of fulfilment for most people.

Working with service users to help them have a sense of achievement is a key part of applying the value base. It is tempting to undertake tasks *for* people you work with because you are keen to care for them and because you believe that you can make their lives easier. Often, however, you need to hold back from directly providing care or carrying out a task, and look for ways you can enable service users to undertake the task for themselves.

For example: it may seem easier, less painful and quicker for a service user if you put on his or her socks or stockings. But this would reinforce the fact that they are no longer able to undertake such a simple task for themselves. Time spent in providing a 'helping hand' stocking aid, and showing them how to use it, means that they can put on their own clothing and instead of feeling dependent, they can have a sense of achievement and independence.

Stocking aid

Sometimes you need to realise that achievement is relative to the circumstances of the individual. What may seem an insignificant act can actually be a huge achievement for a particular individual. Someone recovering from a stroke who succeeds in holding a piece of cutlery for the first time may be achieving something that has taken weeks or even months of physiotherapy, painful exercise and huge determination. The first, supported steps taken by someone who has had a hip replacement represent a massive achievement in overcoming pain, fear and anxiety.

Try it out

Think about some of the achievements in your life. Note them down in the order of their importance to you. You may be surprised to find that some of the achievements which seem the smallest are actually the most important in your life. If possible, sit down with a colleague or friend and try to explain why the achievements on your list are important. If you are not able to discuss this with anyone else, make notes instead.

Developing and maintaining a sense of achievement

Supporting people by encouraging and recognising their achievements is one of the best parts of being a professional carer. Sometimes you may need to spend time in guiding service users and encouraging them in order for them to achieve something. For example:

- You may need to steady someone's hand while they write a thank-you note, but it is far better that you spend time doing this rather than write it for them.
- You could accompany a service user on many trips round the supermarket, and eventually wait in the car park while he or she goes in alone.
- You could demonstrate to a service user with poor motor control how to create pictures by painting with the fingers.

If you want a real insight into the process of celebrating achievements which may seem small to others but have huge significance, ask the parent of any disabled child!

Make sure that you always recognise and celebrate achievements. Think about it – whenever you have achieved something, you usually wanted to share it with someone. Your enthusiasm and recognition are important to your service users.

Setting goals

Beware of situations where either you or the service user are setting out to achieve the impossible. If you tried to stop smoking and go on a diet at the same time, you would be setting yourself up for failure! Try to move service users gently away from unachievable goals, or try to get them to break down the goals into 'bite-size chunks'.

A service user recovering from a spinal injury may say 'I will be back at work in three months.' This is not a goal which should be dismissed, but it is certainly one which needs to be modified. With support and encouragement, such a goal can be broken down into achievable stages, such as: 'I will walk down the corridor with support in six weeks'.

When you are working with service users where there are goals of this nature which have to be broken down into smaller parts, you must always:

- check with the relevant professionals that goals are appropriate for the service user's physical condition (physiotherapist, doctor, speech therapist, etc.)
- plan and agree with the service user, carers and family what the goals are and how they will be achieved
- assist if necessary to monitor progress and achievement
- readjust and modify goals in the light of progress
- celebrate and recognise achievement.

Activity 1.2.1 Achievement

Take a real or imaginary service user and look at a simple achievement. Think of the ways you can encourage and recognise the achievement. Then take a different real or imaginary service user and look at a more complex, longer-term goal. Think of how you can assist to break this down into achievable stages. Make notes or a chart to show how you have worked or could work with a service user.

1.3
Recognise and work with constraints and conflicts

Constraints and conflicts created by living with others

Most care settings, whether residential or providing day-care services, involve living, sharing and working with others. Any situation which involves close and prolonged contact with others has the potential to be difficult. You only have to think about the day-to-day conflicts and difficulties which arise in most families to realise the issues involved when human beings get together in a group.

Disagreements between service users, particularly in residential or day-care settings, are not unusual and you may well find yourself being called on to act as referee. The conflicts can range from disputes over particular chairs or TV channels, to political disagreements or complaints about the behaviour of others. Conflict resolution is never an easy task, wherever you are and however large or small a scale you are working on. However, there are some basic guidelines to follow:

- remain calm and speak in a firm, quiet voice – do not raise your voice
- make it clear that physical violence is completely unacceptable
- make it clear that verbal abuse will not be tolerated
- listen in turn to both sides of the argument – don't let people interrupt each other
- look for reasonable compromises which involve both parties in winning some points and losing others
- make it clear to both sides that they will have to compromise – that total victory for one or the other is not an option.

A wide range of difficulties can arise. They can be about behaviour which is unacceptable and causes distress to others, such as loud music or shouting. They can also be about matters which seem trivial but can cause major irritation when people live together, such as the way someone eats, or the fact that they mutter out loud as they read the newspaper.

Sometimes conflicts can arise about behaviour which is not anyone's fault, but is the result of someone's illness or condition. For instance, sometimes people experiencing some forms of dementia may shout and moan loudly, which may be distressing and annoying to others. Some people may eat messily or dribble as the result of a physical condition, which may be unpleasant and upsetting for those who share a table with them. These situations require a great deal of tact and explanation. It is simply not possible for the individuals concerned to stop their behaviour, so those around them have to be helped to understand the reasons and to cope with the consequences.

Activity 1.3.1 Resolving conflicts

Think about the types of arguments and disagreements which arise in your work setting. If you have been involved in helping to resolve them, make a note of what you did and how effective it was. If another member of staff was involved, note down the actions he or she took and if these were effective. See if you can work out why some actions were effective. If they were not, see if you can work out why they failed.

Constraints and conflicts while working with colleagues

In any care setting, it is not only the service users who have to be together for long periods of time – the staff have to learn to work together too. This may be the first time you have worked in a team with colleagues, or you may have moved to a new team which will function differently from the last place you worked. Each team is different!

Teams take time to learn to work well together. They go through various stages as they settle down, and every time a new team member arrives, things change. Not everyone will share the same views about how tasks should be undertaken and about the right course of action on every occasion. Much will depend on how well the team is managed. However, there are some ground rules that can be applied in most situations, and these will help you make sure that you can work well with others.

- Find out the ways in which decisions are reached and the team members who should be included.
- Always ask for advice and clarify anything you are not sure about.
- Do not assume that everything is the same in every workplace.
- Recognise that every team member, regardless of his or her role and status, has an essential contribution to make.
- Value the input of all colleagues and recognise its importance.
- Make sure that the way you work is not increasing the workload of others or hindering them in carrying out their own work.

Most workplaces have a means of decision making. There could be planning and review meetings where decisions are made about service provision. Staff meetings may be the forum for making decisions about general practice matters, or there may be specific staff development and training meetings for sharing best practice. Organised meetings run by a line manager or supervisor are the best place for discussing differences about practice or decisions about a particular service user; here, everyone has the chance to have a say and to take account of a range of views from other team members. A well-run staff group should also be able to reach agreement on the best course of action and make sure that all the relevant views are taken into account.

Take an example where there is a disagreement between staff members about the extent to which a service user is able to undertake his or her own care. One member of staff may see that it is important to protect the service user from risk, while another feels that the service user's independence should be encouraged. It is essential that both these views are acknowledged as being equally valid and important, and that a compromise is reached which will leave both workers feeling they have made a contribution to the final actions agreed.

Because of the nature of care work, there are not always hard and fast rules about the details of the best way to provide care. There are basic principles and values which underpin everything, and there are some specific areas of practice which are based on research and evidence, but much of what we do is open to discussion and debate and there is always room to explore new approaches and attitudes.

Activity 1.3.2 Working with colleagues

Write a case study of about half a page about a particular problem or issue with a service user you have worked with, or – if you prefer – use an imaginary situation. Make some notes in bullet-point form about how you approached the situation and why.

Now think about a colleague you work with who would approach the same situation in a different way. If you don't know your colleagues well enough yet, think of a friend or previous colleague and make some notes about what he or she would have done.

Now note down the positive aspects of each of the approaches.

1.4

Promote anti-discriminatory practice

Anti-discriminatory practice is a vital part of the value base. Unless you, as a care worker, work in an anti-discriminatory way, then it is not possible to implement the value base. In order to be able to practise in a way which opposes discrimination, you must first understand the main concepts involved. You are likely to find that you have come across these ideas before, but perhaps not in these terms or in this context. You will need to understand the terms, because you will hear them used throughout the care and related sectors, and they have important implications for your practice.

Stereotyping	Stereotyping is happening when whole groups of people are assumed to be the same. It is often present when you hear phrases like 'These sort of people all ...' 'Old people love a sing song' or 'black people are good athletes' or 'gypsies are all dirty and up to no good' are all stereotyping remarks.
Labelling	Slightly more complex than stereotyping, labelling happens when someone thinks the factor which people have in common is more important than the hundreds of factors which make them different. For example, the remark 'We should organise a concert for the elderly' makes an assumption that being older is what is important about the people concerned, and that somehow as you grow older your tastes become the same as all other people your age. It would be much better to say 'We should organise a concert for older people who like music from the shows' or ' We should organise a concert for older people who like opera', etc.
Discrimination	Discrimination means treating people less favourably because they have a certain feature or characteristic, over which they have no control. Disabled people find it hard to get a job because employers are reluctant to take them on – they discriminate against disabled people. Research has also shown that people with Asian names or from certain areas are

	told that job vacancies have been filled even though they have not. Disabled people are often unable to go to concerts or eat in the restaurants they want to because there are no suitable facilities for them.
Anti-discrimination	This means positively working to eliminate discrimination. It is about more than being against the idea of discrimination. You must ensure through your practice that you protect service users from discrimination by identifying it and taking steps to get rid of it or reduce it wherever you can.

For example, when weekly menus are being planned at a day centre, if no account is taken of the religious and cultural needs of all the service users, you should raise the issue at a staff meeting and suggest changes. |
| **Oppression** | Oppression is the experience people have when they are discriminated against. People who are oppressed are being prevented from receiving equal treatment and exercising their rights. People who are oppressed often lose self-esteem and find it difficult to see a way to change the treatment they are subjected to. |
| **Anti-oppression** | This is about the practical steps you can take to counteract oppression. In your work setting you will need to make sure that service users have all the information and support they need to understand the rights they have and how to exercise them. This may mean finding out about what they are entitled to and the ways in which they can be helped, setting up appointments for them and providing written information. It can also mean offering emotional support. It is important to recognise when people are being oppressed and denied their rights, either by another individual or by an organisation. You must work to challenge this, or support service users in challenging it for themselves. |

Find examples of different aspects of anti-discriminatory practice. The examples can be from work, from other parts of your life, or from fiction (a book, film or TV programme). For each example look at what you can learn about working in a way which is anti-discriminatory.

Your day-to-day practice and attitudes are important in how effective your anti-discriminatory practice will be. There is little point in challenging stereotyping in support of a service user, and then returning to your own work setting ready to organise all the 'ladies' for a sewing afternoon!

Challenging your own prejudices and attitudes can be difficult, but you need to spend some time checking out your own behaviour, and making sure that you are not guilty of some of the discriminatory behaviour you have been challenging in others.

Exploring your own behaviour is never easy, and you need good support either from your supervisor or close friends to do it. You may be upset by what you find out about some of your attitudes, but knowing about them and acknowledging them is the first step to doing something about them.

As a care worker, it will be easier to make sure that you are implementing the value base effectively if you are confident that you have looked at your own practice and the attitudes which underpin it.

Foundation standard 2
Communicate effectively

Being able to communicate with service users, colleagues and other professionals is an essential 'building block' of the skills you must develop in order to work as a professional in care. Every aspect of the work involves communication.

It is not possible to become an effective worker in care if you do not understand, and put into practice, the basic principles which govern the ways human beings communicate.

You also need to learn about how to make and use records, so that information can be handled efficiently.

What you are going to learn about:

- how to encourage people to communicate
- how to listen effectively
- how to use physical contact effectively
- how to overcome barriers to communication
- ways of making and keeping useful records.

2.1
Encourage communication

What motivates people to communicate?

In general, human beings like to live with other human beings. Most of us are sociable creatures who want to reach out to other people around us. Very few humans lead completely solitary lives. People live and communicate in a range of different groups and communities, for example:

- families
- neighbourhoods
- workplaces
- schools and colleges
- interest/activity groups
- commercial settings
- users of professional services.

The type and level of communication between people is very different, depending on the circumstances. Some communications are personal and very intimate. These are usually with people to whom we are very close.

Other communications are for a wider audience and are aimed at groups of people.

Communication can be formal.

Communication can be completely informal.

Hey – guess what!

Try it out

Over a period of just one day, keep a record of the people you communicate with. Next to each name, write down the type of communication. You may find that most of your communication is informal, or mostly formal. For most of us, it will be a mix of the two.

There are many reasons why people want to communicate with others. We will examine some of these reasons in the following pages.

Meeting basic needs

The earliest communication that most of us make is to ensure survival. Babies cry so that they will be supplied with food and warmth. Their cries are designed to alert the mother to the needs of the baby.

Although the way we use communication becomes more sophisticated as we grow older, wanting to have basic needs met is still an important reason why people need to communicate.

For example, you need to communicate with others if:

All of these reasons are related to meeting different kinds of human needs.

Activity 2.1.1 Why people communicate

Think about a recent communication involving a service user. What was the purpose of the communication ? Why did the service user want to communicate with you? Check if it was for one of the reasons in the diagram above. Set out your answer like this.

1. Description of a communication by a service user:
2. The reason why the service user needed to communicate:

When you work, it is important to think about when, how and why people may want to communicate, and to make sure that you give them the opportunity and encouragement they need. Of course, not everyone needs encouragement to communicate – some do it only too well and too often – but you need always to be aware that some service users and their families may find it difficult to express what they want to say. An encouraging attitude from you can help people feel relaxed and at ease.

Ways to encourage people to communicate

Now that you have a clearer picture of why people need to communicate, you can think about how you can help them to do so. Being encouraging and making it easy for people to talk is not only about using words, and saying 'Please feel free to talk to me about anything at all.' You will need to say that, but also to make communication possible in other ways. Feeling at ease and able to say something to someone needs more than just being told that it is OK to talk. In order to encourage people to communicate, you also need to make sure that:

- people are in the right setting – not in a crowded and noisy place for example, especially if they need to discuss personal matters
- it is clear from your actions that you have time for them – do not stand looking at your watch, or in the doorway
- you are in a position where you can easily hear what they are saying
- you look interested and responsive to what they are saying
- it is possible for the service user to communicate in the way which is easiest for him or her – this may be in a different language, or it may be in writing, by using electronic or synthetic voice communication, by signing or any other means of communication comfortable for the service user.

Try it out

Think about a time when you have found it very hard to say something you wanted or needed to say. This can often happen with people we see as being in authority, such as doctors, teachers or bank managers. Try to remember why it was difficult to communicate. Think about the attitude of the person you were speaking to – was he or she in a hurry, or looking uninterested? Was his or her attitude discouraging? Note down the reasons why, then think about how each of those difficulties could have been overcome if the person you were communicating with had behaved differently. Try to be clear about the changes in the person's behaviour which would have made a difference to you.

2.2

Listen effectively

Communication is a two-way process. This may sound obvious, but a great deal of communication is wasted because only one of the parties is communicating. Think about setting up communication between two radios – when communication is established, the question is asked 'Are you receiving me?' and the answer comes back 'Receiving you loud and clear'. Unfortunately, human beings don't do this exercise before they talk to each other!

If no one is listening and receiving the information a person is trying to communicate, it is just a waste of time. Learning how to listen is a key task for anyone working in care.

You may think that you know how to listen and that it is something you do constantly. After all, you are listening to all sorts of noises all day long – but simply hearing sounds is not the same thing as actively listening.

Try it out

Think about a time you have talked to someone you felt was really interested in what you were saying and listening carefully to you. Try to note down what it was that made you so sure the person was really listening. Did the fact that you thought he or she was really listening to you make it easier to talk?

Foundation Care Handbook for the TOPSS Standards

For most people, feeling that someone is really listening to them makes a huge difference to how confident they feel about talking. You need to learn about ways in which you can show people you are listening to what they are saying.

Using body language

Although you may think that you do most of your communicating by speaking, you may be surprised to learn that over 80% of what you communicate to others is understood without you speaking a word. Body language, or non-verbal communication, is the way in which we pick up most of the messages people are trying to give us – and some that they're not!

The way in which you use your body can convey messages about:

- your feelings
- your attitudes
- your intentions
- your interest
- your concern
- your attention.

The messages are made clear by such things as facial expression, or maintaining eye contact; sitting forward when you are listening, or having an open and relaxed posture.

Your body language will let people know that you are really listening to what they are saying. Practise your listening skills in just the same way you would practise any other skill – you can learn to listen well.

Always:

- look at the person who is talking to you
- maintain eye contact, without staring
- nod your head to encourage the person to talk and show that you understand
- use 'aha', 'mm' and similar expressions to indicate that you are still listening
- lean slightly towards the person who is speaking – this indicates interest and concern
- have an open and interested facial expression, which should reflect the tone of the conversation – happy, serious, etc.

Using verbal communication

Body language is one key to effective listening, but what you say in reply is also important. You can back up the message that you are interested and listening by checking that you have understood what has been said to you. Using phrases beginning 'so ...' to check that you have got it right can be helpful. 'So ... it's only since you had the fall that you are feeling worried about being here alone.' 'So ... you were happy with the service before the hours were changed.'

You can also use phrases such as 'So ... what you mean is ...' or 'So ... what you are saying is ...'

While people are talking you can also use short, encouraging phrases to show concern, understanding or sympathy. Phrases such as 'I see', 'Oh dear', 'Yes', 'Go on' all give the speaker a clear indication that you are listening and want him or her to continue.

Using questions

Sometimes questions can be helpful to prompt someone who is talking, or to try to move a conversation forward. There are two different kinds of questions. Questions that can be answered with just 'yes' or 'no' are **closed questions**. 'Would you like to go out today?' is a closed question.

An **open question** needs more than 'yes' or 'no' to answer it. 'What is your favourite kind of outing?' is an open question. Open questions usually begin with:

- what
- how
- why
- when
- where.

Depending on the conversation and the circumstances, either type of question may be appropriate. For example, if you are encouraging someone to talk because he or she has always been quiet, but has suddenly begun to open up, you are more likely to use open questions to encourage him or her to carry on talking. On the other hand, if you need factual information or you just want to confirm that you have understood what has been said to you, then you may need to ask closed questions.

Check your learning

What type of question is each of the following?

- 'Are you feeling worried?'
- 'What sort of things worry you?'
- 'Do you want to join in the games tonight?'
- 'Is your daughter coming to visit?'
- 'Why were you cross with Marge this morning?'
- 'Were you cross with Marge this morning?'
- 'What have you got planned for when your daughter comes to visit?'
- 'Do you live here alone?'
- 'How do you feel about living alone?'

One of the main points to remember when listening is that whatever you say, there should not be too much of it! You are supposed to be listening, not speaking. Some DON'T's for good listening:

- Don't interrupt – always let people finish what they are saying, and wait for a gap in the conversation.
- Don't give advice – even if asked. You are not the person concerned, so you cannot respond to questions such as 'If you were me …'. Your job is to encourage people to take responsibility for their own decisions, not to tell them what to do!
- Don't tell people about your own experiences. Your own experiences are relevant to you because they teach you about the person you are, but your role is to listen to others, not talk about yourself.
- Don't ever dismiss fears, worries or concerns by saying 'that's silly …' or 'you shouldn't worry about that.' People's fears are real and should not be made to sound trivial.

Think about two particular occasions when you have been involved in communicating with service users. Write a brief description of the circumstances, and then write notes on how you showed the service users that you were listening to them. If you have not yet had enough experience of working with service users to be able to think of two occasions, think about times when you have listened effectively to a friend or relative and write about that instead.

2.3
Use physical contact effectively

Physical contact between people is tremendously important. For many people one of the hardest features of being left alone when a partner dies is that they can go for weeks or months with no one touching them. Physical contact as part of communication can be encouraging and supportive, although careful consideration must be given to when, and with whom, it is appropriate to use physical contact.

When you work in care you will find that physical contact can be important in a range of ways:

It's OK – I'll stay until you are settled in

Physical contact can reassure service users

You will need to be touched by service users who need to be guided

You will need to use touch to guide some service users to feel objects

If service users are distressed or unhappy, physical contact can provide comfort and support

You may need to stop someone from walking into a dangerous situation

Touch can also give encouragement and support

Physical contact as a means of communication

Some service users rely more heavily than others on touch as a means of communication and you will need to think about this regardless of the area of care you work in. For example, people who do not have sight may not always know that you are there unless you touch them. Physical touch is also vital for people who are deaf or hard of hearing – it is often the only way of attracting their attention. People who are without speech or who have speaking difficulties will often use touch as a means of communication and it is appropriate for you as the care worker to respond if that is the way they want to communicate.

You should never assume, though, that this is what service users want. Not everyone who is deaf may want you to touch them to attract their attention; not all those who are not sighted are happy for, or need, you to touch them to let them know that you are there. You will need to establish a set of 'ground rules' at the outset when you begin to work with a service user, and you will need to include the use of physical contact in the discussions. This is likely to be a discussion with the service user, but it may be that the service user has an advocate to assist in explaining his or her wishes.

When physical contact can be inappropriate

All kind of factors can make physical contact inappropriate for some service users. Not everyone enjoys being touched. Some people are prepared to be touched only by a few particular people and find any other touches unwelcome and unacceptable. You will need to be sensitive to this, and look for signals which indicate that someone is uncomfortable. Signals can be:

- going quiet
- moving away
- looking uncomfortable or embarrassed
- changing the subject abruptly.

Service users may be unhappy with being touched for all sorts of reasons. This could be to do with age – some older people may feel uncomfortable about particular types of physical contact. For example, an older woman may not wish to be touched by a male carer.

There are often cultural barriers to physical contact. For instance, Muslim women are not allowed to be touched by any males other than their husband, and this includes doctors and carers. You must make it your job to check that you are observing a service user's cultural practices. If you are not sure, ask – either the service user or his or her friend or relative. Do not assume that touch will be acceptable without checking.

Some service users who are survivors of abuse or violence may find physical contact very hard to deal with. Their experience of touch has been emotionally and physically devastating, and they find it very unwelcome to be touched by a carer. You should always be aware that this may be a reason, so it is important to be sensitive to the reaction you get to physical contact, and to respond accordingly.

Try it out

Think of three people you have touched in the past 24 hours. Were they family? friends? colleagues? service users? Note down the types of physical contact you had with them. See if there are any types of contact which are common to all the people you touched. Do you use the same types of physical contact with service users and your family? Colleagues and friends? Service users and friends? See if there is a clear pattern linking the types of contact and the closeness of the relationship.

Dealing with aggression

Another circumstance in which physical contact is not appropriate is when you are dealing with a service user who is violent or physically aggressive. Intervention in this type of situation should be by speaking firmly and clearly, but use of physical contact is not advisable. It is very easy, in this situation, for such contact to be misinterpreted and be seen as an attack or an assault. You will also place yourself at risk of injury or assault.

Physical contact with service users is important. It conveys caring and concern, but it also needs thought. Be sure that you always consider whether it is appropriate for both the person and the situation.

Activity 2.3.1 and 2.3.2 Physical contact

Note down two situations in which physical contact could be valuable and two situations in which it would be inappropriate. Note your reasons for each situation.

2.4

Promote communication where there are barriers and challenges

Identifying the main barriers to communication

Not all communication is straightforward. On many occasions there are barriers to overcome before any effective communication can take place. Barriers can exist for all sorts of reasons – some to do with the physical environment, some to do with the background and circumstances of the service user, and some to do with the approach of the care worker.

The first barriers to check out are those which you could be creating yourself. You may think that you are doing everything possible to assist communication, but be sure that you are not making it difficult for service users to understand what you say.

As a professional care worker, you will use all kinds of quick ways to speak with colleagues. Using initials (acronyms) to refer to things is one of the commonest ways in which professionals use shortcuts when talking to each other. Some acronyms are commonplace and others are particular to that work setting. Often, particular forms or documents are referred to by initials – this is obviously useful in one workplace, but not in any others! Referring to medical conditions, types of medication, therapies or activities by initials or by using professional jargon can make it difficult for service users to understand, because these are words they don't use every day. Many of us would have difficulty following the explanation of a mechanic as to what was wrong with a car if he or she used only technical words and jargon. Similarly, service users and their families may have difficulty following care workers' communication. It is not very unusual to hear something like this:

Right – we've checked your BP – that's fine, your Hb came back OK so that means we can do an RF down to Gill our OT – she'll come and see you then fill out a 370 – that'll go to social services who'll send a CCM out to do an assessment and formulate a plan – OK?

It would have been more useful to say:

Your blood pressure is fine. The blood test showed that you're not anaemic, so that means that you're well enough for us to contact Gill, the occupational therapist. She will see you and assess what you can do and what help you may need. After that she'll contact social services and one of the community care managers will visit you to talk about the help and support you would like to have.

It takes a little longer, but saves time and confusion in the long run.

Some barriers to communication can be caused by failing to follow some of the steps towards good communication. If people are not given the proper space and time to say the things they want to say, or are sitting in a noisy or crowded place, with care workers who sit too far away or invade their personal space, they can be discouraged from talking. Poor or unwelcoming body language is another barrier which you need to avoid.

Service users with particular communication needs can often face barriers in communicating with care workers. You will need to take steps to reduce or overcome these barriers in order to make it possible for you to communicate with some service users. For example, you may have to make arrangements for an interpreter to be provided if a service user speaks a language you cannot understand. You may need to make sure that a signer is available if that is the form of communication used by a service user who is deaf, and you cannot sign. Service users who have dementia or are confused may take a long time to understand what you are communicating and you will need to lengthen the time you allow for talking to them.

The table below gives some suggestions for actions you may take to encourage good communication.

Communication difference	Encouraging actions
Different language	• Smile • Wear a friendly facial expression • Use gestures • Use pictures • Show warmth and encouragement – repeat their words with a smile to check understanding
Hearing impairment	• Speak clearly, listen carefully, respond to what is said to you • Remove any distractions and other noises • Make sure any aids to hearing are working • Use written communication where appropriate • Use signing where appropriate and understood • Use properly trained interpreter if high level of skill is required
Visual impairment	• Use touch to communicate concern, sympathy and interest • Use tone of voice rather than facial expressions to communicate mood and response

	• Do not rely on non-verbal communication, e.g. facial expression or nodding head • Ensure that all visual communication is translated into something which can be heard, either a tape or somebody reading
Confusion or dementia	• Repeat information as often as necessary • Keep re-orientating the conversation if you need to • Remain patient • Be very clear and keep conversations short and simple • Use simple written communication or pictures where they seem to help
Physical disability	• Ensure that surroundings are appropriate and accessible • Allow for difficulties with voice production if necessary • Do not patronise • Remember that some of the service user's body language may not be appropriate
Learning difficulties	• Judge appropriate level of understanding • Make sure that you respond at the right level • Repeat things as often as necessary • Remain patient and be prepared to keep covering the same ground • Be prepared to wait and listen carefully to responses

Try it out

Think of a service user with whom there are barriers to communication. Identify the barriers and note them down. Suggest how you could overcome each one.

Responding to challenging behaviour

People's behaviour is as much a means of communication as their facial expression or their words. If people are behaving in an unusual way or presenting you with a challenge, this tells you something of how they feel about what is going on around them.

You may find yourself dealing with behaviour which is new to you, or behaviour you have seen before but with service users you have never met. The types of behaviour which can make communication difficult can vary in different settings. Each workplace will have policies to deal with challenging behaviour and you must make sure that you are familiar with them. You should also discuss with your supervisor the types of behaviour you are likely to come across in your workplace.

Many care workers have to deal with verbal abuse or aggression from service users. This may be related to anger and frustration or it may be related to the medical condition of the service user. Clearly, reasonable communication is not possible with someone who is being aggressive and abusive, and the situation needs to be calmed before communication can begin.

The basic rule is to follow the policies of your workplace in dealing with the particular behaviour, but do not be concerned about trying to communicate effectively until you have dealt with the behaviour and the situation is calm enough for communication to be possible.

Dealing with people who are violently angry is difficult and, as a general rule, should be undertaken by highly experienced and skilled staff. If you find you are faced with this situation you should speak loudly (without shouting), firmly and clearly. Do not ask questions or enter into a discussion – you should issue short, clear instructions such as 'Stop shouting – now', 'Move away from Jim', 'Go and sit down', 'Go into my office' and so on. This type of short, firm instruction has a chance of defusing the situation and restoring enough calm for the problems to be investigated.

Violent situations

There are some situations when verbal abuse and aggressive behaviour turn to violence, and this places you and service users at risk. You should never try to deal with a violent situation alone – you should always get help. Your workplace will have policies and you should follow these closely. If you find yourself in a situation which has become increasingly aggressive and you believe that there is a risk of violence, then you must get help immediately. Depending on your situation, you may not be able to leave the room – if you possibly can get out safely, then you should do so in order to summon help and take yourself out of the risky situation. See Unit 3 for more on avoiding the risk of violence.

2.5

Understand the principles of good record keeping

The purposes of records

Regardless of the setting you work in, you are likely to have to keep records of the work you do. Often, completing records can feel like a chore, and something to be done in the quickest possible way. Knowing why you are completing records and what they are to be used for can often help to make the whole exercise seem more purposeful.

Broadly, records are likely to be used for a range of purposes:

- passing on information about the service user to others who will provide care when you are off duty
- passing on information to others who will meet different care needs
- recording statistical information for your own organisation – this will help to monitor and review the present work and to plan future services
- recording statistical information for national organisations – this is used to plan budgets and policies for future services
- providing an accurate legal record of the care provided to an individual service user. This record can be accessed by the service user and can be used in any legal dispute concerning care.

Every record you complete will have a specific use. It may sometimes feel as if organisations have forms for the sake of it, but they will all have a purpose. Make sure that you ask your supervisor about all the records you keep and what they will be used for.

You also need to know where each record is kept. Many will be kept together with the service user's notes or case file, and that will be kept in a particular location. Many filing systems are alphabetical, but some large organisations, such as hospitals, use a numbering system because names are quite often the same. A hospital which filed medical notes under names and had provided services for twelve people called Christopher Williams would soon run into problems.

You must make sure that you know how the filing system works in your workplace, where you can find each record and where you should return it.

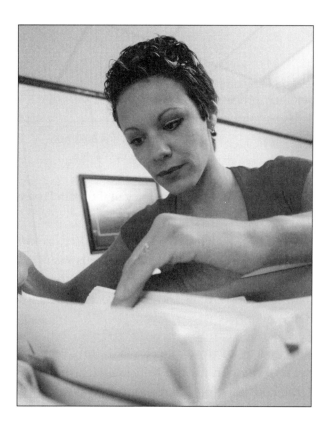

Issues of confidentiality

Another key question you need to ask about records is who has access to them. There are certain principles which apply. All organisations in health and care have a policy that the minimum possible number of people should have access to records, and this is on a 'need-to-know' basis. Personal information on service users should be respected as confidential, and not freely shared with anyone just because they happen to work for your organisation or because they happen to be in a similar job role to yours in another setting. People who want to access records for a service user must have a good reason, and one that is in the interests of the service user, for doing so.

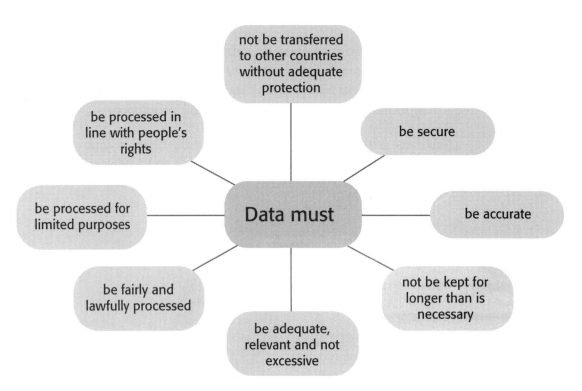

The principles of the Data Protection Act 1998

Information which is held on computer, as most now is, is covered by the Data Protection Act 1998. This also sets out a series of principles which are a legal requirement for all those responsible for the maintenance of data and records. The principles are shown in the diagram above.

A formal set of principles for handling confidential information has been developed for the National Health Service. These are called the Caldecott Principles and they are also appropriate for other health and care settings. The principles are concerned with 'patient identifiable information' – that is, information which reveals or could reveal the identity of a particular service user.

The Caldecott Principles

Principle 1 – Justify the purpose
Every proposed use or transfer of patient identifiable information within or from an organisation should be clearly defined and scrutinised, with continuing uses regularly reviewed by an appropriate guardian.

Principle 2 – Don't use patient identifiable information unless it is absolutely necessary
Patient identifiable information items should not be used unless there is no alternative.

Principle 3 – Use the minimum necessary patient identifiable information

Where use of patient identifiable information is considered to be essential, each individual item of information should be justified with the aim of reducing identifiability.

Principle 4 – Access to patient identifiable information should be on a strict need-to-know basis

Only those individuals who need access to patient identifiable information should have access to it and they should have access only to the information items that they need to see.

Principle 5 – Everyone should be aware of their responsibilities

Action should be taken to ensure that those handling patient identifiable information, both clinical and non-clinical staff, are aware of their responsibilities and obligations to respect patient confidentiality.

Principle 6 – Understand and comply with the Law

Every use of patient identifiable information must be lawful. Someone in each organisation should be responsible for ensuring that the organisation complies with legal requirements.

Activity 2.5.1 and 2.5.3 Purpose and confidentiality of records

Make a list of the types of records you will use in your workplace, and their purposes. Make notes about how confidential they are, and who should have access to them.

Making sure records are relevant and useful

No matter how carefully records are stored and filed, they are of no use if they cannot be understood, either because the person recording them wrote in such a way that they cannot be read – there are many millions of illegible medical case notes! – or because they are written in such a way that the meaning is not clear. Records should be clear, accurate and to the point. Consider the examples on the next page:

> Mrs P had a bad night.

Too little information

> Mrs P had a bad night. It began when I found her crying about 10 p.m. She said she had been thinking about her husband. I thought she seemed a bit hot, so I made her a cup of tea and got her to sit in the lounge for a while before she went to bed. After about half an hour, I managed to get her to go to her room and I went with her . . .

Too much irrelevant information

> Mrs P had a bad night because:
> a) she was distressed about her husband
> b) she wandered out of her room about 2 a.m. crying again
> c) unable to settle despite further cocoa
> d) wandered into Mr W's room at 5.30 believing he was her husband
> She will need to be closely observed today. Any further confused episodes should be logged.

Clear, helpful. Gives a short picture of problems overnight, and suggests action for next day

Issues of accountability

Remember, you are responsible (accountable) for what you write, so make sure that you can justify it and that you are accurately recording what you have seen or heard for yourself. The facts you are writing down should be recorded accurately and in a way that can be checked. If you want to record information which you have heard from someone else, then make sure you state clearly where the information came from.

Activity 2.5.2 and 2.5.4 Record keeping

Write an imaginary record of the care given to a service user, over a period of seven days. Mark the points in the record where you have included information which will be helpful to colleagues. Write a note explaining what the service user could learn about her care if she requested access to the records.

Foundation standard 3
Develop as a worker

Given the right circumstances, human beings have the potential to develop throughout their lives; people who make the most of every opportunity to learn and develop become self-confident, self-assured and fulfilled. The workplace provides many development opportunities, from improving learning about the job to knowing how to recognise and deal with risks associated with the work.

In order to achieve the outcomes of this standard you will need to show that you understand how you can develop at work, how to use supervision effectively, how to minimise the risks linked with the work you do, and how to maintain health and safety.

What you are going to learn about:

- how to develop yourself as a care worker
- how to keep safe and healthy.

3.1
Worker development

Learning from work practice

Everything you do at work is part of a process of learning. Even regular tasks are likely to be important for learning because there is always something new each time you do them. A simple task like taking a service user a hot drink may result in a 'lesson for today' if, for example, you find that the service user tells you that he or she doesn't want tea, but would actually prefer coffee this morning, thank you! You will have learned the valuable lesson of never making assumptions about everything remaining the same – and will have proved the truth of the saying: 'Use your head to save your legs'.

Learning from working is also about using the huge amount of skill and experience which your colleagues and supervisor will have. Not only will they be able to pass on knowledge and advice to you, but you have the perfect opportunity to discuss ideas and talk about day-to-day practice in the service you are delivering.

Finding time to discuss work with colleagues is never easy – everyone is busy and you may feel that you should not make demands on their time. But most colleagues and supervisors are happy to talk about good and bad practice and to give guidance and advice whenever they can, so you must develop the skill of timing. When you have a question to ask, don't choose the moment when your supervisor has a desk overflowing with statistical returns and shift rotas, nor the moment when one of the service users has just tipped a full commode over the bedroom floor! Use supervision time or quiet periods, and take the chance to discuss situations which have arisen, problems you have come across or new approaches you have noticed other colleagues using.

Make notes over the next week about periods of time which seem to be quiet and may offer a good opportunity to talk to a senior colleague. You will also have supervision time with your manager. When you have worked out the good times, take the initiative and raise a question about work you have been doing. It may be something quite straightforward such as 'How do you always manage to keep everything so neat when you do a bedbath?' or more complex such as 'Can you explain why it is OK to let Mr G go out to the shops by himself? It seems such a risk.'

Try this with different experienced colleagues – you'll be surprised at how much you will learn.

Getting it right and getting it wrong

Everyone makes mistakes – they are one way of learning. It is important not to waste your mistakes, so if anything has gone wrong, make sure you learn from it. Discuss problems and mistakes with your supervisor, and work out how to do things differently next time. You will develop as a result of learning from situations which have not worked out the way you planned. However, it is important that you consider carefully why things turned out the way they did and think about how you will ensure that they go according to plan next time. Unfortunately, there are real people on the receiving end of our mistakes in care, and learning how not to do it again is vitally important.

Talking to colleagues and supervisors is equally useful when things work out really well. It is just as important to learn why something worked, so that you can repeat it. In order to think about learning from your work, it is helpful to be clear about what you want to achieve and how. Look at the case study below.

Case study

Mr J has been very unhappy since the death of his wife just over a year ago. He has stopped going out and has no interest in meeting other people or becoming involved in any activities. You have to provide domiciliary care to Mr J, and you decide to support him in re-establishing contact with other people. You make a plan so that you can check how well this has worked.

What to achieve (the aim):

Improve Mr J's social contacts

Goals which help to measure success (objectives):

Mr J to agree to meet local organiser of Age Concern

Mr J to attend St Chad's luncheon club

How to do it (method):

1. Talk to him about meeting the organiser and secure his agreement

2. Arrange the meeting at his home

3. Be there for the meeting

4. Be positive and encouraging

5. Offer to occompany him for his first visit to the luncheon club

6. Arrange transport for his first visit

7. Go with him

This type of plan will help you see if you are achieving your aim at each stage, by checking your progress. You will then know at which point something has not worked and can ask for help if necessary from your colleagues and supervisor. It will also help you to know when something has gone well and your plan is working. Don't simply pat yourself on the back! Explore why your work went well. Use your supervision time and opportunities to talk with experienced colleagues.

Make good use of training/development opportunities

Personal development is to do with developing the personal qualities and skills that everyone needs in order to live and work with others, such as understanding, empathy, patience, communication and relationship-building. It is also to do with the development of self-confidence, self-esteem and self-respect. If you look back on the ways in which you have changed over the past five years, you are likely to find that you are different in quite a few ways. Most people change as they mature and gain more life experience. Important experiences such as changing jobs, moving home, illness or bereavement can change people. It is inevitable that your personal development and your professional development are linked – your personality and the way you relate to others are the major tools you use to do your job. Taking advantage of every opportunity to train and develop your working skills will also have an impact on you as a person.

Professional development is to do with developing the qualities and skills that are necessary for the workplace. Examples are teamwork, the ability to communicate with different types of people, time management, organisation, problem solving, decision making and, of course, the skills specific to the job.

Continuous professional development involves regularly updating the skills you need for work. You can achieve this through attending training sessions both on- and off-the-job, and by making the most of the opportunities you have for training by careful planning and preparation.

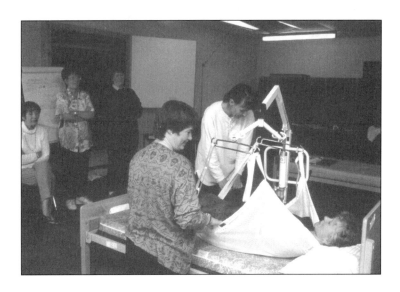

How to get the best out of training

Your supervisor will work with you to decide on the types of training that will benefit you most. This will depend on the stage you have reached with your skills and experience. There would be little point, for example, in taking a course in micro-surgery techniques if you were at the stage of having just achieved your First Aid certificate! It may be that not all the training you want to do is appropriate for the work you are currently assigned to – you may think that a course in advanced therapeutic activities sounds fascinating, but your supervisor may suggest that a course in basic moving and handling techniques is what you need right now. You will only get the best out of training and development opportunities if they are the right ones for you at the time. There will be opportunities for training throughout your career, and it is important that you work out which training is going to help you to achieve your goals.

Personal development plans

It is a requirement of many organisations that their staff have personal development plans. A personal development plan is a very important document as it identifies a worker's training and development needs and, because the plan is updated when the worker has taken part in training and development, it also provides a record of participation.

A personal development plan should be worked out with your supervisor, but it is essentially your plan for your career. You need to think about what you want to achieve, and discuss with your supervisor the best ways of reaching your goals.

There is no single right way to prepare a personal development plan, and each organisation is likely to have its own way. However, it should include different development areas, such as practical skills and communication skills, the goals or targets you have set – such as training in moving and handling, or learning to sign – and a timescale for achieving them. Timescales must be realistic – do not, for example, aim to learn to sign in six weeks, or even six months. But you could aim to complete moving and handling training within six weeks.

When you have set your targets, you need to review how you are progressing towards achieving them – this should happen every six months or so. You need to look at what you have achieved and how your plan needs to be updated.

How to use training and development

Every formal training opportunity you take part in should be in your plan. You should work with your supervisor to prepare for the training and to review it afterwards. You may want to prepare for a training session by:

- reading any materials which have been provided in advance
- talking to your supervisor or a colleague who has attended similar training, about what to expect
- thinking about what you want to achieve as a result of attending the training.

Make the most of training by:

- taking a full part and asking questions about anything you don't understand
- collecting any handouts and keeping your own notes of the training.

Think about how to apply what you have learned by discussing the training with your supervisor later. Review the ways in which you have benefited from the training.

Different ways of learning

Formal training and development is not the only way you can expand your knowledge and understanding. There are plenty of other ways to keep up progress towards the goals you have set in your personal development plan. Not everyone learns best from formal training. Other ways people learn are from:

- being shown by more experienced colleagues – this is known as 'sitting next to Nellie'
- reading textbooks, journals and articles
- following up information on the Internet
- asking questions and holding professional discussions with colleagues and managers.

Write down the different ways of learning that you have experienced. Have you, for example, studied a course at college, worked through a distance-learning programme or attended hands-on training sessions? Tick the learning methods which have been the most enjoyable and most successful for you.

How could you use this information about how you best like to learn in order to update your workplace skills?

Here is a checklist of ways of learning that you might find useful:

- watching other people
- asking questions and listening to the answers
- finding things out for yourself
- going to college and attending training courses
- studying a distance-learning course or a course on the Internet.

Activity 3.1.2 Training and development

Think about the last training or development session that you took part in and write a short report.

- Describe the preparations you made beforehand so that you could benefit fully from it.
- Describe what you did at the session; for example, what and how did you contribute, and what did you learn? Do you have a certificate to show that you participated in the session? Do you have a set of notes?
- How did you follow up the session? Did you review the goals you had set yourself, or discuss the session with your supervisor?
- Describe how you have used what you learned at the session. For example, how has the way you work changed, and how have your clients and colleagues benefited from your learning?

Using supervision effectively

It is sometimes difficult to take a step back and look at whether your working practices have improved as a result of training, development and increasing experience, so it is very important to seek out and act on feedback from an appropriate person, usually your supervisor.

Asking for feedback on your performance is not always easy – and listening to it can be even harder! All of us find it difficult to hear feedback at times, especially if we are being told we could do better.

However, you should learn to welcome feedback – try to think of it as looking in a mirror. You probably never go out without looking in the mirror to check how you look. How will you know how your work performance is looking, if you haven't asked anyone who is in a position to tell you?

Your supervisor's role

Your supervisor will support and advise you in your work and make sure that you know and understand:

- your rights and responsibilities as an employee
- what your job involves and the procedures your employer has in place to help you carry out your job properly
- the philosophy of care where you work – that is, the beliefs, values and attitudes of your employer regarding the way service users are cared for, and how you can demonstrate values of care in the way you work
- your career development needs – the education and training requirements for the job roles you may progress into, as well as for your current job.

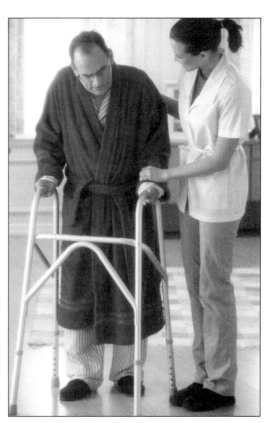

Try it out

Ask your supervisor whether there is a policy or plan at work on the supervision of staff.

If there is, read it and note down what it covers, for example how you will be supervised, how often you can expect to be formally supervised, and what kinds of things your supervisor will be able to help you with in your work role and career.

If there is no plan for supervision, make a list of the things on which you would like your supervisor's support, and agree a time and place to discuss these items with him or her.

Think about a situation when you have used supervision well and it has been helpful in improving your work. Make some notes which describe the situation, and ask your supervisor to discuss them with you.

3.2
Keeping safe and healthy

Risks to your safety and well-being

Working in care does have risks associated with it. It certainly doesn't qualify as one of the world's more dangerous occupations, but you need to be aware of the risks you may be exposed to and what you and your employer are able to do about reducing those risks.

The Health and Safety at Work Act 1974

This Act describes the health and safety responsibilities of employers and workers in all workplaces.

The responsibilities of employers are to:

- ensure that the workplace remains healthy and safe
- provide workers with health and safety information, training and supervision.

The responsibilities of workers are to:

- always follow basic safety rules
- co-operate with the employer to promote health and safety
- report health or safety hazards promptly.

In addition, everyone – employers, workers and the general public – has a responsibility not to interfere with or misuse anything provided for the purpose of health and safety.

If you work for an organisation that employs five or more workers, your employer should have a written health and safety policy. Find out where the policy is kept and note down which parts of the policy directly relate to you.

Ask your supervisor where the risk assessment documents for your workplace are kept. Read the documents and make a list of those that relate directly to the work that you do.

Violence and aggression

People who receive care services are often distressed, angry, ill or confused. As a result, they may lash out or respond aggressively to what may seem to be a straightforward situation. You need to be aware when a normal situation is changing into one where there may be risks involved. You can tell when a person is becoming distressed by noticing:

- changes in the voice – it may be raised or at a higher pitch than usual
- changes in facial expression – this could be scowling, crying, snarling
- changes in the eyes – pupils could be dilated and eyes open wider
- body language demonstrating agitation, or an aggressive stance leaning forward with fists clenched
- reddening of the face and neck
- excessive sweating
- changes in breathing patterns – the person may breathe faster than normal.

If you do find yourself in a situation where you fear you may be attacked, or where you are being verbally abused, you need to take steps to try to calm the situation if you can, and to keep yourself safe if you cannot.

Calming a situation

Try to respond in ways least likely to promote further aggression:

- use your listening skills, and appear confident (but not cocky)
- keep your voice calm and at a level pitch
- do not argue
- do not get drawn into prolonged eye contact

- attempt to defuse the situation with empathy and understanding. For example, 'I realise you must be upset if you believe that George said that about you. I can see that you're very angry. Tell me about what happened.'

Be prepared to try a different approach if the first one doesn't work. Always make sure that an aggressor has a way out of the situation that maintains dignity, both physically and emotionally.

Dealing with violence or aggression

Take some common-sense precautions: make sure you know where the exits are; move so that the aggressor is not between you and the exit; notice if there is anything which could be used as a weapon, and try to move away from it; make sure that the aggressor has enough personal space, and do not crowd him or her.

If you are faced with a violent situation, you should try to remain calm (even though that is easier said than done!) and not resort to violence or aggression yourself.

It is often the case that a simple technique like holding up a hand in front of you, as if you were directing traffic, and shouting 'Stop' may deflect an attacker or stop him or her long enough for you to get away. You should remove yourself from the situation as speedily as possible.

If there are other, vulnerable people at risk, you must decide whether you can summon help more effectively from outside or inside the situation.

If you decide to remain you must summon help at once. You should do one of the following:

- press a panic alarm or buzzer, if one is provided
- shout 'help' very loudly and repeatedly
- send someone for help
- call the police or security officers, or shout for someone else to do so.

Do not try to be a hero – that is not your job.

The risk of violence is the most dramatic of the risks you face, but it is certainly not the most common.

Reducing the risk of infection

Your everyday work in care will bring you into contact with a host of micro-organisms which can pass on infection and disease. Cross-infection is the term which describes the passing of infection from one person to another. This can occur in a range of ways, such as:

- from the hands of a health or care worker moving from one service user to another
- from the clothes of a health or care worker
- through inadequate decontamination of instruments or equipment between use with one service user and another
- through breathing in droplet infection or dust infection from the air
- from linen or surfaces which have been inadequately cleaned.

It is important to remember that people who are already vulnerable, because they are elderly or very young, or have some other illness or infection, are far more likely to be infected than somebody who is healthy and fit. You need to take extra care because most of the service users you are dealing with are likely to be those who are particularly susceptible to infection. The aim of cleaning, disinfecting and sterilising an environment is to minimise the risk of cross-infection. Your personal hygiene practice is one of the most significant factors in reducing the risk of infection being spread.

Some of the basic ways in which you can reduce the spread of infection are shown below.

Wear gloves

- *When?* Any occasion when you will have contact with body fluids (including body waste, blood, mucus, sputum, sweat or vomit), or when you have any contact with anyone with a rash, pressure sore, wound, bleeding or any broken skin. You must also wear gloves when you clear up spills of blood or body fluids or have to deal with soiled linen or dressings.
- *Why?* Because gloves act as a protective barrier against infection.
- *How?* Check gloves before putting them on. Never use gloves with holes or tears. Check that they are not cracked or faded. Pull gloves on, making sure that they fit properly. If you are wearing a gown, pull them over the cuffs. Take them off by pulling from the cuff – this turns the glove inside out. Pull off the second glove while still holding the first, so that the two gloves are folded together inside out. Dispose of them in the correct waste disposal container and wash your hands.

Wash your hands

- *When?* Before and after carrying out any procedure which has involved contact with an individual or with any body fluids, soiled linen or clinical waste. You must wash your hands even though you have worn gloves. You must also wash your hands before you start and after you finish your shift, before and after eating, after using the toilet and after coughing, sneezing or blowing your nose.
- *Why?* Because hands are a major route to spreading infection. When tests have been carried out on people's hands, an enormous number of bacteria have been found.
- *How?* In running water, in a basin deep enough to hold the splashes and with either foot pedals or elbow bars rather than taps, because you can re-infect your hands from still water in a basin, or from touching taps with your hands once they have been washed. Use the soaps and disinfectants supplied. Make sure that you wash thoroughly, including between your fingers.

Wear protective clothing

- *When?* You should always wear a gown or plastic apron for any procedure which involves bodily contact or is likely to deal with body waste or fluids. An apron is preferable, unless it is likely to be very messy, as gowns can be a little intimidating to service users.
- *Why?* Because it will reduce the spread of infection by preventing infection getting on your clothes and spreading to the next person you come into contact with.
- *How?* The plastic apron should be disposable and thrown away at the end of each procedure. You should use a new apron for each individual you come into contact with.

Tie up hair

- *Why?* Because if it hangs over your face, it is more likely to come into contact with the individual you are working with and could spread infection. It could also become entangled in equipment and cause a serious injury.

Clean equipment

- *Why?* Because infection can spread from one person to another on instruments, linen and equipment just as easily as on hands or clothes.

- *How?* By washing large items like trolleys with antiseptic solution. Small instruments must be sterilised. Do not shake soiled linen or dump it on the floor. Keep it held away from you. Place linen in proper bags or hampers for laundering.

Dealing with waste at work

Another essential part of reducing the risk of infection is to deal with waste properly. Your workplace will have its own system, but it is likely to be similar to the one shown in the table below.

Type of waste	Method of disposal
Clinical waste – used dressings	Yellow bags, clearly labelled with contents and location. This waste is incinerated.
Needles, syringes, cannulas ('sharps')	Yellow sharps box. *Never* put sharps into anything other than a hard plastic box. This is sealed and incinerated.
Body fluids and waste – urine, vomit, blood, sputum, faeces	Cleared and flushed down sluice drain. Area to be cleaned and disinfected.
Soiled linen	Red bags, direct into laundry – bags disintegrate in wash. If handled, gloves must be worn.
Recyclable instruments and equipment	Blue bags, to be returned to the Central Sterilisation Services Department (CSSD) for recycling and sterilising.

Keeping yourself safe

If you work in the community and visit service users in their own homes, you need to take additional precautions to make sure that you are not at risk when you are working. The precautions may sound like common sense, but they are essential and you should make sure that you follow them at all times. All of the previous guidelines on infection control and dealing with aggressive situations apply, but you should also make sure that you:

- always leave details of where you are going and what time you expect to return

- carry a personal alarm and use it if necessary
- work with a colleague in situations which may be risky
- do not tackle any aggressive or violent person – get out of the situation and raise the alarm.

Risks to you from working practices

If your work involves looking at a computer screen for long periods (more than an hour at a time), you should check with your supervisor what the arrangements are for you to have regular breaks. Sitting in poorly adjusted chairs or undertaking repetitive activities such as inputting computer data without the right equipment can cause you to suffer from strains and muscle injuries. Your employer is required to assess all these possible risks to you and will have put processes in place to protect you.

Keeping fit and healthy through good diet and appropriate rest

Working in care is a demanding job and you cannot afford to take risks with your own health. Some simple rules will provide you with a basic plan for maintaining a healthy lifestyle.

A good diet

There are five main food groups. If we eat a variety of foods from these five groups in the proportions recommended by health professionals, we can be confident of having a nutritionally balanced diet – one that contains all the nutrients we need to stay healthy.

Although water isn't a nutrient, our bodies need it for a number of reasons. We need it to produce sweat which helps control body temperature, to get rid of waste material (in urine and faeces) and for blood and other body fluids. We should aim to drink at least two pints of water a day.

Food group	Proportion of daily diet	Examples of foods
Bread, other cereals & potatoes	We should aim for this food group to make up about one third of what we eat every day.	Bread, chapattis, rice, pasta, breakfast cereals, maize, millet, green bananas, potatoes, beans, lentils.

Food group	Proportion of daily diet	Examples of foods
Fruit & vegetables	We should aim for this food group to make up about one third of what we eat every day. We should try to eat 5 portions of fruit and vegetables every day.	Fresh, frozen and canned fruit and vegetables.
Meat, fish & alternatives	We should aim for this food group to make up about one sixth of what we eat every day.	All types of meat (preferably low fat) and fish; eggs, beans, nuts, soya.
Milk & dairy foods	We should aim for this food group to make up about one sixth of what we eat every day.	Milk, cheese, yoghurt (preferably low fat).
Foods containing fat and foods containing sugar	These foods should be eaten only occasionally and in small amounts.	Butter, margarine, mayonnaise, oily salad dressings, crisps, sweetened drinks, ketchup, sweets, biscuits, cakes, puddings.

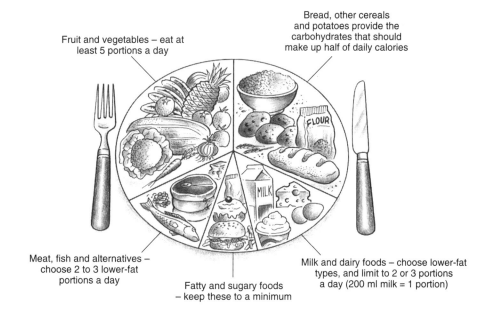

Fruit and vegetables – eat at least 5 portions a day

Bread, other cereals and potatoes provide the carbohydrates that should make up half of daily calories

Meat, fish and alternatives – choose 2 to 3 lower-fat portions a day

Fatty and sugary foods – keep these to a minimum

Milk and dairy foods – choose lower-fat types, and limit to 2 or 3 portions a day (200 ml milk = 1 portion)

The proportions suggested here are only guidelines, because the amount of nutrients that individuals need varies depending on factors such as their age, lifestyle and occupation. For example, someone who leads a very active lifestyle will need more energy-giving foods, such as bread and cereals, than someone who has a deskbound job and takes little exercise; and a growing child will need more body-building foods, such as meat, fish or nuts, than an elderly person.

Check your learning ✓

Think about your typical daily diet. Bearing in mind your age, level of activity and job, decide whether you are eating a balanced diet and make a note of how you could change what you eat to ensure that it is balanced.

Also check your fluid intake (not counting coffee or alcohol!). Are you drinking enough water?

Activity and exercise

Many people who work in care have plenty of physical activity at work – some days it feels as if you have walked miles and lifted Olympic weights! However, the human body thrives on physical exercise, and any activity which makes your heart and lungs work harder is good for you. While increasing your activity levels can mean doing something new to you, it can also mean doing just what you usually do but in a more energetic way. Run upstairs instead of walking, or walk upstairs instead of taking the lift! Walk to the shops instead of taking the bus or car. Dancing, swimming, cycling, playing tennis and attending low-impact aerobics classes all offer a relatively painless way of increasing your levels of activity. Activities like these can be great fun when they involve a group of friends, and they are a marvellous way to meet new people and to relax.

Strange as it may seem, the more active you become, the more energy you will seem to have! People who are physically active on a regular basis say that they:

- have more energy
- have more stamina or staying power
- are stronger and leaner (more toned)
- have an improved posture, shape and appearance
- have more self-confidence and feel better about themselves
- feel more relaxed and rested in general
- sleep better.

Health professionals report that people who are more active have a lower risk of:

- circulatory and heart disease
- respiratory problems
- high blood pressure
- stroke
- osteoporosis (brittle bone disease)
- mental health problems.

Rest and sleep

One of the benefits of exercise is that it promotes rest and sleep, which are very important for everyone. When we are resting or asleep:

- our muscles relax
- our blood pressure, pulse rate and body temperature fall
- our digestive system becomes more active so that our meals can be properly digested and our body tissues can become topped up with nutrients.

If we are deprived of rest and sleep, we can

- suffer memory loss
- become irritable and depressed
- lose our ability to think straight and carry out daily tasks.

Try it out

How do you sleep? Well? Or do you find it difficult to get off to sleep or to stay asleep? Keep a record of how you sleep over a period of about a week. Can you see a link between how well you sleep and the kinds of activities you do when you are awake?

Sleeping is not the only way of resting and relaxing. Rest your body and your mind by:

- switching off from work with a good book or film
- relaxing with friends
- walking or taking other gentle exercise
- playing sport
- just sitting and daydreaming.

These are useful ways of renewing your mental energy as well as the physical energy you need to do your job well.

Activity 3.2.2 Diet and relaxation

Write a plan for yourself for a typical (and health-conscious) day, which:

- describes what you will eat and drink, and explains your choices
- describes the physical activity you will do
- describes what you will do for relaxation and explains why you choose to relax in this way
- describes how and when you will rest (including sleep) and explains why you need to rest.

Stress

Stress can be beneficial – for example, some people work better under pressure and a certain amount of stress can focus your energy and be quite stimulating. If you enjoy the rides at theme parks you will understand how exhilarating stress can be! However, too much stress can damage your health.

What causes stress?

Stress means different things to different people. The kind of things that can cause stress include:

- work pressures
- being in debt
- having relationship problems
- interrupted sleep.

Stress is believed to be one of the major causes of time off work and of staff turnover. Stress at work can be caused by:

- poor working relationships
- the type of work that has to be carried out, especially in social care

- the hours spent at work, especially for shift workers
- a lack of career progression opportunities
- a fear of redundancy or retirement.

Recognising stress

Stress can show itself in a number of ways. Emotionally, stress can cause people to feel:

- tense, irritable, angry
- depressed, anxious, tearful, worthless
- unable to cope, to concentrate or make decisions
- tired and stretched to the limit
- uninterested in everything, including sex.

Physically, stress can cause:

- headaches and migraines
- circulatory disorders such as high blood pressure, heart attacks, strokes
- respiratory disorders such as asthma and chest pains
- digestive disorders such as ulcers
- menstrual problems
- increases in infections, such as cold sores and colds.

Try it out

Think of an occasion when you felt very stressed. Make a list of the feelings/emotions and physical symptoms you had at the time.

Methods of dealing with stress

We all have our own ways of coping with stress, but sometimes our coping mechanisms can make the situation worse! Things we should avoid doing in response to stress are:

- drinking alcohol
- smoking
- compulsive eating.

Behaviours like these might make us feel better at the time, but in the long run they can be very damaging to our health.

Positive ways to deal with stress include the following.

- Physical activity, for example going for a walk, doing some gardening, or even punching a pillow. Physical activity uses up the extra energy our bodies produce when we are stressed.

- Talking things over, for example with a friend or your supervisor. Chatting about a problem often helps you identify what the real issues are, and how to deal with them.
- Doing something to take your mind off the problem, for example going to the cinema, or reading a magazine. Escaping from a problem for a while enables you to come back to it with a clear head, and makes you feel more able to tackle things.
- Using relaxation techniques – activities in which you learn to control your breathing. These can help to release the muscular tension that goes hand-in-hand with stress.

- Organising your time well. Don't take on more than you can handle, and do things in the order of their importance.
- Learning to shrug things off. Raise your shoulders and lower them a few times – this uses up energy, leaving you feeling more relaxed; it also helps you get things into perspective. How important is what is causing the stress anyway?

Support, advice and guidance

If you are suffering from symptoms of stress which persist, and you can see no way forward, you should seek help.

Family and friends are usually the first people we would look to for support. They have either experienced stress themselves or know someone who has been in your position, and can offer support and help.

If your stress is associated with work, talk things through with your supervisor. Some organisations employ individuals whose role includes counselling people with problems and guiding them in finding solutions.

If the symptoms of stress are seriously affecting your life, or if they have gone on for a long time, you should consult your GP, who can treat your physical symptoms and perhaps refer you to a suitably qualified therapist or counsellor.

Massage or alternative therapies such as reflexology and aromatherapy can also be very valuable in helping to relieve stress.

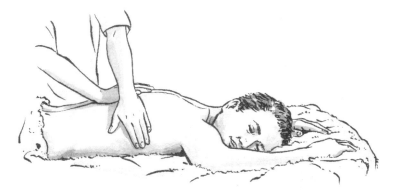

There are also voluntary organisations and telephone help-lines that you can contact; and a mass of literature, from leaflets through to text books, is available in your local library or bookshop, full of information about how to cope with stress.

Activity 3.2.3 Stress

Write a description of a care worker (real or imaginary) who is suffering from stress. Describe his or her symptoms, and suggest what could be done to help relieve the stress.

Foundation standard 4

Recognise and respond to abuse and neglect

For many people, starting work in care means coming to terms with the fact that some service users will be subjected to abuse by those who are supposed to care for them. For others it will not be the first time that they have been close to an abuse situation, either through personal experience or previous professional involvement.

Regardless of previous experience, coming face to face with situations where abuse is, or has been, taking place is difficult and emotionally demanding. Knowing what you are looking for, and how to recognise it, is an important part of ensuring that you are making the best possible contribution to protecting service users from abuse. Taking the right steps when faced with an abusive situation is the second part of your key contribution to service users who are, or have been, abused.

The forms of abuse which you will need to be aware of and to understand are abuses suffered by service users at the hands of someone who is providing care for them. This standard is not about abuse by strangers, which needs to be dealt with in the same way as any other crime.

What you are going to learn about:

- how to understand the nature of abuse
- how to understand the nature of neglect
- how to recognise the signs and symptoms of abuse
- how to recognise the signs and symptoms of neglect
- how to understand when and how to respond to abuse or neglect.

4.1

Understand the nature of abuse

Abuse takes place where one person exercises power in a harmful and negative way over another. The abuser can be anyone who has caring responsibilities for the service user – this includes professional as well as informal carers. A wide range of people can provide different types of care for a service user, whether he or she is an adult or a child. The table shows some examples:

Professional/formal carer	Informal carer
Care assistant	Parent
Social worker	Step-parent
Nurse	Son/daughter
Doctor	Sister/brother
Health visitor	Grandchild
Physiotherapist	Grandparent
Occupational therapist	Other relative
Ambulance crew	Friend
Hospital porter	Neighbour
Health centre staff	Volunteer
Probation officer	
Teacher	
Nursery worker/nanny	

People who are providing care are likely to be in a powerful position in relation to the service user. Some service users are more vulnerable than others, and this is, to some extent, related to their individual needs and circumstances. Someone who is frail, confused and lives alone is potentially vulnerable to some forms of abuse such as physical, sexual or emotional abuse. Someone who has profound learning difficulties or is confused is also more vulnerable to financial abuse.

People who abuse others do so as a result of misusing their power. Instead of recognising that the strength they have in relation to the service user is a positive thing which should be used to provide support and protection, they use their position in order to exercise power for their own purposes, and control others in a way which is damaging and dangerous.

Naturally, if you are providing care for someone, you are likely to be physically stronger and more powerful than that person. You may be able to exert power because of your professional role and the tasks you undertake for the service user, and it is also possible that your role places you in a position of authority which may intimidate the service user. It may be that you have greater intellectual ability than the service users you care for, or that they are in a position where they are totally dependent on you for their day-to-day personal care. Whatever the nature of the role which places a carer in a position of authority and power, the misuse of that position is a betrayal of trust and service users must be protected from it.

The forms of abuse

Abuse can take many forms. These are usually classified under five main headings:

- physical
- sexual
- emotional
- financial
- institutional.

Abuse can happen to any service user, regardless of his or her age or service needs. Child abuse is the most well-known and well-recognised type of abuse, but all service user groups can suffer abuse. Abuse of the elderly and of those with learning difficulties, sensory impairment or physical disabilities is just as common, but often less well recognised.

Physical abuse

Any abuse involving the use of force is classified as physical abuse. This can mean:

- punching, hitting, slapping, pinching, kicking, in fact any form of physical attack
- burning or scalding
- restraint such as tying people up or tying people to beds or furniture
- refusal to allow access to toilet facilities
- deliberate starvation or force feeding
- leaving service users in wet or soiled clothing or bedding as a deliberate act, to demonstrate the power and strength of the abuser
- excessive or inappropriate use of medication
- a carer causing illness or injury to someone he or she cares for in order to gain attention (this is called 'Munchausen's syndrome by proxy').

Sexual abuse

Sexual abuse, whether of adults or children, is also abuse of a position of power. Sexual activity is abusive when informed consent is not freely given. It is important to recognise the difference between the freely consenting sexual activity of adults who also happen to be service users, and those situations where abuse is taking place because of the powerful position of someone who is supposed to be providing care.

Children can never be considered to give informed consent to any sexual activity of any description. For many adults, informed consent is not possible because of a limited understanding of the issues. In the case of other adults, consent may not be given and the sexual activity is either forced on the individual against his or her will or the individual is tricked, bribed or coerced into it.

Sexual abuse can consist of:

- sexual penetration of any part of the body with a penis, finger or any object
- touching inappropriate parts of the body or any other form of sexual contact without the informed agreement of the service user
- sexual exploitation
- exposure to, or involvement in, pornographic or erotic material
- exposure to, or involvement in, sexual rituals
- making sexually explicit comments or references which provide sexual gratification for the abuser
- making threats about sexual activities.

Emotional abuse

All the other forms of abuse have an element of emotional abuse, because they cause distress. Any situation which means that a service user becomes a victim of abuse at the hands of someone he or she trusted is, inevitably, going to cause emotional pain. However, some abuse is purely emotional, and there are no physical, sexual or financial elements involved. This abuse can take the form of:

- humiliation, belittling, putting down
- withdrawing or refusing affection
- bullying
- making threats
- shouting, swearing
- making insulting or abusive remarks
- racial abuse
- constant teasing and poking fun.

Financial abuse

Many service users are very vulnerable to financial abuse, particularly those who may have a limited understanding of money matters. Financial abuse, like all other forms of abuse, can take a range of forms, such as:

- stealing money or property
- allowing or encouraging others to steal money or property
- tricking or threatening service users into giving away money or property
- persuading service users to take financial decisions which are not in their interests
- withholding money, or refusing access to money
- refusing to allow service users to manage their own financial affairs
- failing to support service users in managing their own financial affairs.

Institutional abuse

Institutional abuse is not confined to the large-scale physical or sexual abuse scandals of the type regularly publicised in the media. Of course this type of systematic and organised abuse does go on in residential and hospital settings, and must be recognised and dealt with appropriately so that service users can be protected. However, service users can be abused in many other ways in settings where they could expect to be cared for and protected. For example:

- service users in residential settings are not given choice over day-to-day decisions such as mealtimes, bedtimes etc.
- freedom to go out is limited by the institution
- privacy and dignity are not respected
- personal correspondence is opened by staff
- the setting is run for the convenience of staff, not service users
- excessive or inappropriate sedation/medication are given
- access to advice and advocacy is restricted or not allowed
- complaints procedures are deliberately made unavailable.

You can probably begin to see that the different types of abuse are often interlinked, and service users can be victims of more than one type of abuse. Abuse is a deliberate act – it is something which someone actively does in order to demonstrate power and authority over another person. It is also done with the motive of getting some sort of gratification for the abuser.

Activity 4.1.1 Understanding forms of abuse

Abuse takes different forms. Make notes about each of the different forms and give at least two examples of each form of abuse.

4.2
Understand the nature of neglect

Neglect is very different from abuse. Whereas abuse involves a deliberate act, neglect happens when care is not given and a service user suffers as a result. The whole area of neglect has many associated issues and aspects you need to take into account, but there are broadly two different types of neglect:

- self-neglect
- neglect by others.

Self-neglect

Many people neglect themselves; this can be for a range of reasons. Someone may be ill or depressed and unable to make the effort, or not feel capable of looking after themselves. Sometimes people think that looking after themselves is unimportant. Others may choose to live in a different way from most people, and not match up to the expectations of others. Working out when someone is neglecting himself or herself, given all of these considerations, can be very difficult.

Self-neglect can show itself in a range of ways:

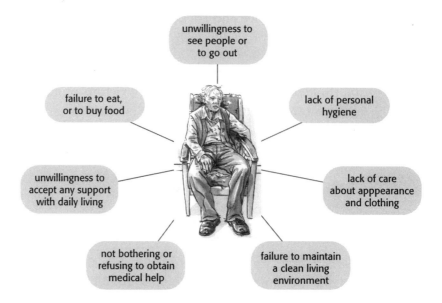

However, what may appear to be self-neglect may, in fact, be an informed choice made by someone who does not regard personal and domestic cleanliness or hygiene as priorities. It is always important to make a professional judgement based on talking with the service user and finding out his or her wishes, before making any assumptions about what may be needed.

Attempting to force someone to accept help with domestic and personal cleanliness, when he or she has made a clear choice to live in an environment which differs from what is generally acceptable, would directly contravene the value base of care work. This value base supports the rights of service users to make choices in respect of their lives (see Unit 1). However, issues can arise when the ways of living chosen by a service user have a direct impact on the lives of others. This is more likely to happen in the community, but it is also possible that such situations can occur in a residential environment, if, for example, a service user refuses to wash.

Situations like these are difficult to deal with, and it is important to think through the reasons why action may be necessary – or why action may seem to be necessary, but may not be justified on further consideration.

It may be hard to imagine the kind of tensions and conflicting views you may come across. Look at the following case study – you could discuss the issues it raises with your colleagues or supervisor.

Case study

B is 75, and he has lived alone since his wife died two years ago. Both he and his wife were academic writers and they were never very sociable or friendly with neighbours. They had no children and did not appear to have any friends. The house and garden had always been dilapidated and very untidy, and this appears to have become worse since B's wife died.

Neighbours contacted Social Services because they felt that B was neglecting himself. He very rarely went out to the shops and appeared very thin and unkempt. When social workers visited him, his house was dirty and there was very little food in the cupboards. He was dirty and his clothes were unwashed. B agreed to be visited by a psychiatrist. She could find no evidence of mental illness – in fact she described B as an intelligent and articulate man. B politely explained to all his visitors that he did not see the point of washing, that he was unconcerned about food and was not bothered if he should die or become ill as a result of his actions.

Check your learning

Ask one of your experienced colleagues, or your supervisor, if he or she can recall a situation where a service user had made a choice about lifestyle which gave others a cause for concern. Ask the following questions:

1. Why was the choice a problem for the professional carers?

2. What are the problems created when service users adopt a risky lifestyle?

3. How was the situation resolved?

Neglect by others

This occurs when either a professional or informal carer is caring for a service user and the care needs of the service user are not met. Neglect can happen because those responsible for providing the care do not realise its importance, or because they cannot be bothered, or choose not, to provide it. As the result of neglect, service users can become ill, hungry, cold, dirty, injured or deprived of their rights. Neglecting someone you are supposed to be caring for can mean failing to undertake a range of care services, for example:

- not providing adequate food
- not providing assistance with eating food if necessary
- not ensuring that the service user receives personal care
- not ensuring that the service user is adequately clothed
- leaving the service user alone
- failing to maintain a clean and hygienic living environment
- failing to obtain necessary medical/health-care support
- not supporting social contacts
- not taking steps to provide a safe and secure environment for the service user.

In some care situations, carers may fail to provide some aspects of care because they have not been trained, or because they work in a setting where the emphasis is on cost saving rather than care provision. In these circumstances it becomes a form of institutional abuse. Unfortunately, there have been residential care homes and NHS Trusts where service users have been found to be suffering from malnutrition as the result of such neglect. Individual workers who are deliberately neglecting service users in spite of receiving training and working in a quality caring environment are, fortunately, likely to be spotted very quickly by colleagues and supervisors.

However, carers who are supporting service users in their own homes are in different circumstances, often facing huge pressures and difficulties. Some may be reluctantly caring for a relative because they feel they have no choice, others may be barely coping with their own lives and may find caring for someone else a burden they are unable to bear. Regardless of the many possible reasons for the difficulties which can result in neglect, it is essential that a suspicion of neglect is investigated and that concerns are followed up so that help can be offered and additional support provided if necessary.

As with self-neglect, it is important that lifestyle decisions made by service users and their carers are respected, and full discussions should take place with service users and carers where there are concerns about possible neglect.

4.3

Recognise the signs and symptoms of abuse

One of the most difficult aspects of dealing with abuse is to admit that it is happening. If you are someone who has never come across deliberate abuse before, it is hard to understand and to believe that it is happening. It is not the first thing you think of when a service user has an injury or displays a change in behaviour. However, you will need to accept that abuse does happen, and is relatively common. Considering abuse should be the first option when a service user has an unexplained injury or a change in behaviour which has no obvious cause.

Abuse happens to children and adults. Victims often fail to report abuse for a range of reasons:

- they are too ill, frail or too young
- they do not have a good level of understanding of what is happening to them
- they are ashamed and believe that it is their own fault
- they have been threatened by the abuser or are afraid
- they do not think they will be believed
- they do not believe that anyone has the power to stop the abuse.

Given the fact that relatively few victims report abuse without support, it is essential that those who are working in care settings are alert to the possibility of abuse and are able to recognise possible signs and symptoms. Signs and symptoms can be different in adults and children and you need to be aware of both, because regardless of the setting you work in you will come into contact with both adults and children. Your responsibilities do not end with the service user group you work with. If you believe that you have spotted signs of abuse of anyone, you have a duty to take the appropriate action.

Signs and symptoms

Information on signs and symptoms of abuse comes with a warning – none of the signs or symptoms is always the result of abuse, and not all abuse produces these signs and symptoms. They are a general indicator that abuse should be considered as an explanation. You and your colleagues will need to use other skills such as observation and communication with other professionals in order to build up a complete picture.

Physical signs of possible abuse in adults

Abuse can often show itself in physical effects and symptoms. These are likely to be accompanied by emotional signs and changes in behaviour, but this is not always the case.

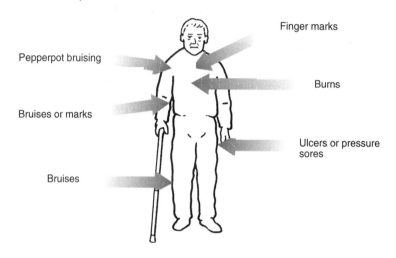

Type of sign/ symptom	Description of sign/symptom	Possible form of abuse indicated
Physical	frequent or regular falls or injuries	physical
Physical	'pepperpot bruising' – small bruises, usually on the chest, caused by poking with a finger or pulling clothes tightly	physical
Physical	fingermarks – often on arms or shoulders	physical
Physical	bruising in areas not normally bruised, such as the insides of thighs and arms	physical
Physical	unusual sexual behaviour	sexual
Physical	blood or marks on underclothes	sexual
Physical	recurrent genital/urinary infections	sexual
Physical	marks on wrists, upper arms or legs which could be from tying to a bed or furniture	physical/sexual
Physical	burns or scalds in unusual areas such as soles of feet, insides of thighs	physical
Physical	ulcers, bedsores or rashes caused by wet bedding/ clothing	physical
Physical	missing cash or belongings, or bank accounts with unexplained or unusual withdrawals	financial
Physical	missing bank account records	financial

Type of sign/ symptom	Description of sign/symptom	Possible form of abuse indicated
Emotional/ behavioural	becoming withdrawn or anxious	all forms of abuse
Emotional/ behavioural	loss of interest in appearance	sexual/physical/ emotional
Emotional/ behavioural	loss of confidence	sexual/physical/ emotional
Emotional/ behavioural	sudden change in response to financial matters	financial
Emotional/ behavioural	becoming afraid of making decisions	emotional
Emotional/ behavioural	sleeping problems	all forms of abuse
Emotional/ behavioural	changes in eating habits	all forms of abuse
Emotional/ behavioural	no longer laughing or joking	all forms of abuse
Emotional/ behavioural	feeling depressed or hopeless	all forms of abuse
Emotional/ behavioural	flinching or appearing afraid of close contact	physical
Emotional/ behavioural	unusual sexual behaviour	sexual

Emotional or behavioural signs of abuse in adults

Any behaviour changes could indicate that the service user is a victim of some form of abuse, but remember that they are only an indicator and will need to be linked to other factors to arrive at a complete picture.

Carer behaviour which should alert you to possible abuse

Sometimes, it is not the behaviour of the service user which is the first noticeable feature of an abusive situation. It can be that the first behaviour you notice is that of the carer. The following are some indications of behaviour which may give cause for concern, although with the usual warning that these are only *possible* indicators of problems:

- reluctance to allow visitors to see the service user
- insistence on being present with the service user at all times
- derogatory or angry references to the service user
- excessive interest in financial accounts or assets
- excessive requests for repeat prescriptions.

Activity 4.3.1 Signs and symptoms of abuse

Go back to the notes you made for the Activity on page 77. Give two examples of possible signs which could alert you to each of the forms of abuse you have identified.

4.4

Recognise the signs and symptoms of neglect

The effects of neglect are similar, whether the neglect is at the hands of others or is self-neglect by the service user. The signs and symptoms give a clear indication that something is wrong and that the situation requires checking. It may be that the service user has made a lifestyle choice in respect of how he or she wishes to live, but this will need to be confirmed. However, it is more likely that service users are neglecting themselves or being neglected because they, or their carer, need support and assistance to ensure that they are not at risk. Any of the following may be a sign that a service user is being neglected:

- being dirty, unkempt or smelly
- wearing dirty or damaged clothing
- being regularly hungry
- living in a cold environment
- missing medical or other appointments
- having untreated illnesses or injuries
- suffering weight loss
- suffering poor skin condition, sores and rashes
- being isolated and having limited contacts.

4.5

Understand how to respond to abuse and neglect

When you find out, or suspect, that a service user is being abused or neglected, you have a responsibility to take action immediately. Concerns, suspicions and firm evidence all require an immediate response.

There are several situations in which you may find yourself in the position of having information to report concerning abuse or neglect.

- A service user may disclose to you that the or she is being abused or neglected.
- You may have clear evidence that abuse or neglect is happening.
- You may have concerns and suspicions, but no definite evidence.

How to respond to disclosure

The correct term for a service user telling you about abuse or neglect is 'disclosure'. If a service user discloses abuse to you, the first and most important response is **you must believe what you are told.**

This is often harder than it sounds. If you have never been involved with an abusive situation before, it is hard to believe that such cases arise and that this could really happen.

One of the biggest fears of those being abused is that no one will believe them – do not make this fear into a reality.

You must reassure the person, whether an adult or a child, that you believe what you have been told. Another common fear of people who are being abused is that it is somehow their own fault – so you must also reassure them that it is not their fault and that they are in no way to blame for what has happened to them.

When a service user discloses abuse or neglect to you, try not to get into a situation where you are having to deal with a lot of detailed information. After reassuring the service user that you believe him or her, you should report the disclosure immediately to a senior colleague and hand over responsibility. This is not always possible because of the circumstances or location in which the disclosure takes place, or because the service user wants to tell you everything once he or she has started disclosing. If you do find yourself in the position of being given a great deal of information, you must be careful not to ask any leading questions – for example, do not say 'And then did he punch you?' Just ask 'And then what happened?' Use your basic communication and listening skills so that the service user knows he or she can trust you and that you are listening. Make sure you concentrate and try to remember as much as possible so that you can record it accurately.

Another common problem which arises with disclosure is that you may be asked to promise to keep the information secret. **You must never make this promise – it is one you cannot keep.**

What you can do is promise that you will tell only people who can help. You may well find yourself in this situation:

If I tell you something will you promise not to tell anyone?

I can't promise that until I know what you are going to tell me.

You mustn't tell anyone. I'll get killed!

I can promise you this – I'll tell only people who can make you safe.

Remember – people disclose abuse because they want it to stop. They are telling you because they want you to help make it stop. You cannot make it stop if you keep it secret.

The most important first step is to ensure that you know the procedures in your workplace for dealing with abuse and neglect. All workplaces will have policies and procedures and it is vital that you are familiar with them and know exactly who you need to report to.

Situations where you have evidence

There may be situations where you have evidence of abuse, either because you have witnessed it happening or because you have other evidence such as bank slips, forged pension books, etc. These situations must be reported immediately to your supervisor, or the person identified in the procedures followed by your workplace for cases of abuse. You should make sure that you provide all the detailed evidence you have, with full information about how you found the evidence and how and where you have recorded it.

Situations where you have concerns

It is more likely that you will not have evidence, but you have noticed some of the signs or symptoms of possible abuse. You must report this as rapidly as you would if you had clear evidence.

It may be tempting to wait until something happens to confirm your suspicions, but do not do this. You may not be aware of it but other people may also have concerns, and only when all the information is put together will a full picture emerge. Think of it like a jigsaw puzzle. It is not possible to see what the picture will be if you have only one or two pieces – you need to contribute your pieces so that, by working together with colleagues, as many pieces as possible can be put in place.

Dealing with institutional abuse

One of the most difficult situations to deal with is institutional abuse, particularly if you believe it is taking place within your own workplace, or elsewhere in your organisation. If you are concerned about possible institutional abuse or neglect you should follow the same procedures as you would for any other abuse or neglect concerns.

- Refer your concerns to your line manager or supervisor.
- If you believe that your manager is involved in some way, or will not take action, report to a more senior manager who you believe will be impartial.
- If you do not feel confident that you can report the abuse to anyone within your workplace or organisation, you should report your concerns to the National Care Standards Commission, who are responsible for ensuring that standards are maintained in all care settings.

Whistleblowing

Reporting your concerns about practice in your workplace is known as 'whistleblowing', and you cannot be victimised for doing this. An Act of Parliament protects you – it is called the UK Public Interest Disclosure Act. The Act came into force on 2 July 1999. It encourages people to 'blow the whistle' about malpractice in the workplace and is designed to ensure that organisations respond by acting on the message, rather than punishing the messenger.

The Act applies to employees reporting crime, civil offences (including negligence, breach of contract, etc.), miscarriage of justice, danger to health and safety or the environment, and the covering up of any of these. It applies whether or not the information is confidential, and extends to malpractice occurring in the UK and any other country or territory.

In addition to employees, it covers trainees, agency staff, contractors, home workers, and every professional in the NHS. The Act means that your employer cannot take any action to victimise you because you have reported genuine concerns.

Recording

Any information you have, whether it is simply concerns, or hard evidence, or a disclosure, must be carefully recorded. You should write down your evidence, or if you are unable to do so for any reason, you should record it on audio tape. It is not acceptable to pass on your concerns verbally without backing this up with a recorded report. Verbal information can be altered and can have its meaning changed very easily when it is passed on. Think about the children's game of Chinese Whispers – by the time the whispered phrase reaches the end of its journey, it is usually changed beyond all recognition.

Your record should be detailed and clear, and should include information about:

- everything you observed
- anything you have been told, but make sure that it is clear that this is not something you have seen for yourself
- any previous concerns you may have had
- what has raised your concerns on this occasion.

P was visited by her son this afternoon. She was very quiet over tea, did not join in conversation or joke with anyone. Just said she was tired when asked what was wrong. Went to her room without going into lounge for the 'seconds evening'. Said she thought the clothes were too expensive and she couldn't afford them. Unusual for her. Similar to incident about a month ago when she said she couldn't afford the hairdresser – again after a visit from her son. Needs to be watched. Is he getting money from her? For discussion at planning meeting.

Write a report on concerns about an abuse situation which could occur in your workplace. Make up the details. State to whom, in your workplace, you would give the report.

Foundation standard 5

Understand the experiences and particular needs of the individuals using the service

People who use care services do so in order to meet a wide variety of needs. Service users' needs are individual and relate to their own circumstances, and will be different even if their circumstances are similar. A range of factors influence the ways in which people respond to the events and situations that affect their lives. One of the most important aspects of working in care is to understand that the ways in which people behave and the needs they have are the product of the ways they live and their own history.

Providing care means taking all of this into account. Organisations planning to deliver services need to make sure that the services provided are responding to the needs of each individual service user. Organisations and workers providing care need to consider all the many aspects of each service user's circumstances in order to ensure that the service is right for that person, and not simply convenient for the organisation or the worker.

What you are going to learn about:

- the nature of person/child-centred services
- the needs of the individual within a person/child-centred service.

5.1

The nature of person/child-centred services

Care planning with the service user at the centre

The process of providing care is something which should be carefully planned and designed to ensure that the service is exactly right for the individual it is meant to be helping. The importance of recognising and valuing the individual differences between people is highlighted by Foundation Standard 1 and the value base applied to all care provision. This is of key importance, not just because it is a right to which all people are entitled in a civilised society, but also because health and well-being responds to emotional factors as much as physical. Service users will benefit if the service they receive is centred around their own needs and the ways in which they wish those needs to be met. Feeling valued and recognised as a person is likely to improve the self-esteem and confidence of service users and thus contribute to an overall improvement in health and well-being.

Try it out

Think of an occasion when you have felt really special – it may have been a special day, such as a birthday, wedding or anniversary, or a special event such as having a baby, or an achievement like winning an award or passing a test. Note down how you felt and try to recall the reasons why you felt special.

When an individual either requests, or is referred for a service, the assessment and planning cycle begins. Throughout the consultation and planning which follows, the individual and his or her needs should be at the centre of the process. The worker who is assessing and planning the way in which services will be delivered will need to make sure that the service user has every opportunity to state exactly how he or she wishes those needs to be met. Some service users will be able to give this information personally. Others will need an advocate who will support them in expressing their views.

The principles of good communication, which were explored in Unit 2, are important in making sure that the service user is fully involved in making plans for the service he or she will receive.

All organisations must ensure that the way in which services are provided allows the opportunity for service users to express their views, and that all those who will play a part in planning and delivering services on an individual level are able to use listening and communication skills in order to allow the service user to participate fully. The consequences of not planning service delivery around the needs of those who receive it can be far reaching. The table below shows some of them.

Need/wish of service user	Ways to meet need	Possible effects of not taking account of need
Food prepared according to religious or cultural beliefs	Ensure that service is provided by people who have been trained to prepare food correctly	Food not eaten so health deteriorates. Other services refused. Food eaten out of necessity but in extreme distress
To maintain social contacts while in residential care	Provide transport to visit friends and for friends to visit	Service user becomes isolated and depressed
Take control of own arrangements for personal care	Discuss and support the planning of direct payments	Service user loses self-esteem and is disempowered

National Minimum Standards

The central theme and underpinning principle of care provision is that the service is centred on the person receiving it, and not on those providing it. Under the Care Standards Act 2000, service providers are monitored and regulated to make sure that services are meeting the needs of the individuals for whom they are provided.

This Act established the National Care Standards Commission, which is the body responsible for implementing the National Minimum Standards across a wide range of care providers. These include:

- care homes
- children's homes
- residential family centres (from 1 January 2003)
- domiciliary care agencies (from 1 January 2003)
- nurses' agencies (from 1 January 2003)
- independent fostering agencies
- voluntary adoption agencies (from April 2003)

It also includes independent healthcare establishments, such as:

- acute hospitals
- mental health hospitals
- hospices
- maternity hospitals or clinics
- abortion clinics
- private doctors
- establishments using the following prescribed techniques and technologies:

- class 3B or class 4 laser
- intense light sources
- dialysis
- endoscopy
- IVF
- hyperbaric oxygen treatment.

In addition, the Commission is responsible for inspecting:

- local authority fostering services
- local authority adoption services
- the welfare arrangements in boarding schools, residential special schools and further education colleges.

You can see that the Commission is responsible for inspecting and regulating many different establishments – over 40,000. Each type of care provider has a set of National Minimum Standards which must be met. These Standards cover most areas of provision and practice, as shown in the table on the next page.

Throughout all the Standards, the emphasis is on the individual nature of the care provided and the choices given to the individuals receiving services. The Standards are a key part of the process of planning and providing care based on individual need, because they provide the minimum basis on which services should be built.

Think of a row of terraced houses. Although every house may look the same from the outside and have exactly the same sized rooms, the same doors, windows, walls and roof – there the similarity ends. If you go inside each house you will find they're as different as the people who live in them. This is the way you should think of the National Minimum Standards. They provide the 'house', the outer framework, but the ways in which they apply to each individual will be different. It is perfectly possible to receive the same standard of service, but receive it in a different way.

Standard	Areas included
Choice of home	• information • contract • needs assessment • meeting needs • trial visits • intermediate care
Health and personal care	• privacy and dignity • dying and death • service user plan • health care • medication
Daily life and social activities	• meals and mealtimes • social contact and activities • community contact • autonomy and choice
Complaints and protection	• complaints procedures • rights • protection
Environment	• premises • shared facilities • lavatories and washing facilities • adaptations and equipment • individual accommodation: space requirements • individual accommodation: furniture and fittings • services: heating and lighting • services: hygiene and control of infection
Staffing	• staff complement • qualifications • recruitment • staff training
Management and administration	• day-to-day operations • ethos • quality assurance • financial procedures • service users' money • staff supervision • record keeping • safe working practice

A holistic approach

One of the essential aspects of planning care services is to have a holistic approach to planning and provision. 'Holistic' means looking at the 'whole' situation. This involves recognising that all parts of an individual's life will have an impact on care needs and that you need to look beyond what you see when you meet him or her for the first time.

A wide range of factors will have an impact on the circumstances which have brought a service user to request social care services. All of the following will directly affect a service user, and they must be taken into account when considering the best way to provide services.

Health

The state of people's health has a massive effect on how they develop and the kind of experiences they have during their lives. Someone who has always been very fit, well and active may find it very difficult and frustrating to find his or her movement suddenly restricted as the result of an illness, such as a stroke. This may lead to difficult behaviour and the expression of anger against those who are delivering services, or the person may become depressed. Alternatively, someone who has not enjoyed good health over a long period of time may be able to adjust well to a more limited physical level of ability, perhaps having compensated for poor health by developing intellectual interests.

Employment

Poor health is also likely to have had an impact on a person's employment opportunities, either making employment impossible at times or restricting the types of jobs he or she could do. Whether or not people are able to work has a huge effect on their level of confidence and self-esteem. Employment may also have an effect on the extent to which individuals have mixed with others and formed social contacts. This may be an important factor when considering the possible benefits of residential care as opposed to care provided in a home environment.

Income levels are obviously related to employment, and these will have an effect on standards of living – the quality of housing, the quality of diet and the lifestyle people are able to have. Someone in a well-paid job is likely to have lived in a more pleasant environment with lower levels of pollution, more opportunities for leisure, exercise and relaxation, and a better standard of housing. It is easy to see how all of this can affect an individual's health and well-being.

Education

People's level of education is likely to have affected their employment history and their level of income. It can also have an effect on the extent to which they are able to gain access to information about health and lifestyle. It is important that the educational level of an individual is always considered so that explanations and information can be given in a way that is readily understandable. For example, an explanation about an illness taken straight from a textbook used by doctors would not mean much to most of us! However, if the information is explained in everyday terms, we are more likely to understand what is being said. Some people may have a different level of literacy from you, so do not assume that everyone will be able to make use of written notes. Some people may prefer information to be given verbally, or recorded on tape.

Social factors

The social circumstances in which a person has lived will have an immense effect on their way of life and the type of care provision they are likely to need. Traditionally, the social classification of society is based on employment groups, but the social groups in which people live include their families and friends, and people differ in the extent to which they remain close to others. The social circumstances of each person who is assessed for care services must be taken into consideration, to ensure that the service provided will be appropriate.

Religious and cultural factors

Religious and cultural beliefs and values are an essential part of everyone's lives. The values and beliefs of the community people belong to and the religious practices which are part of their daily lives are an essential aspect for consideration in the planning of services. Any service provision which has failed to take account of the religious and cultural values of the individual is doomed to fail.

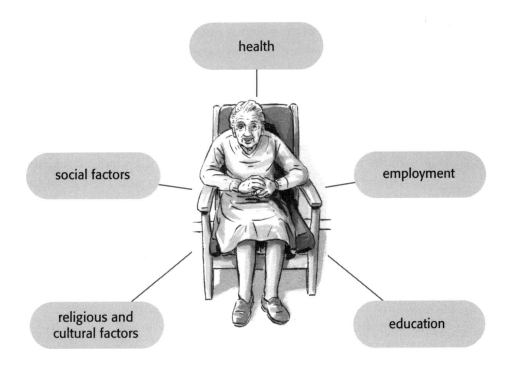

health

social factors

employment

religious and cultural factors

education

Activity 5.1.1 and 5.1.2 A holistic approach

Prepare a list of the different types of service provided by the setting in which you work. Remember to include all the aspects of the service you provide – if you work in residential care, you will need to list all parts of your service such as: social activities, providing food, providing entertainment, personal care, etc. If you work in a service user's own home, you may need to list food preparation, cleaning, personal care, and so on.

Make a note about the factors in a service user's life you would need to take into account in order to provide a holistic assessment of their needs.

Record ways in which you may need to adapt the services you provide because of some of the factors you are taking into account.

When a service cannot be provided

After a holistic assessment has been carried out, ensuring that the service user is the main focus of the planning, it may be found that not all the services which the service user needs or wants can be provided.

There are a number of reasons why this can happen. Usually it involves resources and a lack of funding to provide all the services required. But it can involve other factors too. For example, a service user may have requested a service which is not provided by the organisation. A service user may want, and possibly need, full-time, live-in care in his or her own home, provided by the home carer whom he or she knows. But the agency providing the present home carer may not offer 24-hour care and the home carer may not wish to take up a full-time role.

It could be that a request made by a service user is against the policies of the care organisation – for example, if a service user asked to receive personal care only from carers of a particular race, most care organisations would not be willing to comply with such a request. However, it is quite acceptable to ask for care to be provided by someone of a particular gender.

Funding

Most of the situations where services cannot be provided arise because of a shortage of funding. For their funding, social care organisations fall broadly into three sectors: statutory, voluntary and independent.

Sector	Services include
Statutory	• National Health Service hospitals • council-run residential homes • council-run day-care establishments • council-run domiciliary services • health centres
Voluntary and not-for-profit	• charities such as Help the Aged, Barnardos, NSPCC, Salvation Army, Mencap, etc. • local voluntary groups such as church luncheon clubs, volunteer shoppers, etc. • housing associations providing supported housing
Independent	• private hospitals such as BUPA • private residential care homes • private supported housing

Each of the three sectors is funded in a different way.

- The **statutory sector** is funded through central or local government money provided out of taxes. The allocation of money is always less than it would be possible to spend in an ideal world, and this can mean that services have to be limited or priorities have to be set as to which services or particular service users will take priority.

- The **voluntary sector** is funded largely through charitable donations and fund raising, although some charities also receive grants from the national or European government for specific work. People who work in the voluntary sector are not all volunteers – the professional care workers are all paid. The term 'voluntary' describes the sector and separates it from the sector controlled by government. Many people now prefer to use the term 'not-for-profit' as a way of describing these organisations.
- The **independent sector** is the private sector, where care services are provided for profit as a business. This sector is funded through the fees which are paid, either by individuals or by local authorities who commission their services.

Funding can be a reason for an inability to provide services in all three sectors, although it is more likely to occur in the statutory or voluntary sectors than in the independent sector, where individuals are paying for services.

An organisation's inability to provide the service the user wants can result in unhappiness and dissatisfaction on the part of the service user, and also low morale and concern among staff who may well be frustrated by their inability to meet the needs of their service users.

> *We believe in taking account of the special circumstances of each individual. As from next week, we will be changing our level of service for all those who …*

When there are insufficient resources to meet demand, organisations have to set out rules to decide which services will be available and who will get them. This is always particularly hard to do because the whole value base of person-centred service planning and holistic assessment involves viewing all service users as individuals. It is hard to have to develop rules which are designed to apply to groups of people.

Activity 5.1.3 Ability to provide services

Ask your supervisor about the types of services which your organisation is currently unable to provide because of lack of resources. Note down some of the requests from service users which may have to be refused as a result. Think of one other reason why a request from a service user may be refused.

Having a non-judgemental approach

Being judgemental is not the same as making judgements. The words may sound similar, but the difference is vitally important when providing care services.

As a professional care worker you will have to make judgements all the time. What those judgements are will depend on the nature of your work and the level of responsibility you hold. The judgements may be about the best ways to provide care for an individual service user, or they may be about wider issues relating to a group of service users. You may need to make judgements in an emergency or crisis situation or you may need to make a judgement about the best way to support a relative or carer. Regardless of the level or purpose of your judgement, it is still a decision reached after considering the options and alternatives and reaching a view based on all the evidence.

Being judgemental, however, is something different – it means making assumptions and jumping to conclusions without considering any evidence or relevant information.

Many of the service users you work with may be in situations which are very different from anything you have ever experienced, and their way of life may involve activities or attitudes which you have always believed to be wrong or unacceptable. Being non-judgemental means accepting the ways other people live and understanding that everyone is influenced by their own circumstances. This is not always easy.

For example, if you are someone who believes that families, especially women, have a duty to care for their older relatives, you may find it difficult not to be judgemental about a woman who is refusing to look after her mother and is demanding that social services accept responsibility for providing her care. However, to make a critical judgement about the woman without knowing all the circumstances of her life, her relationship with her mother and other major life events which have affected her, is unprofessional.

You need to be clear that your own outlook has been formed by your own experiences, and that it is no more or less valid than anyone else's viewpoint – it is only one perspective on a situation. Making judgements based on one perspective is dangerous and likely to be wrong. Taking a holistic approach applies to viewpoints and perspectives too – it is important that you give equal value to the different views of others and avoid developing an attitude which fails to take all aspects into account.

5.2 The needs of the individual within a person/child-centred service

The past can have a major impact on service users today. There are two main aspects of history which can have an effect – personal history and social history.

Personal history

All of us have a personal history. Many of the aspects of a service user's life which you have taken into account when making a holistic assessment will form part of their history. Everyone's development has taken a slightly different route and has been influenced by different factors, but all of us have followed broadly the same stages of growth and development throughout our lives. **Development** can be categorised into four different areas:

- physical
- social and emotional
- language
- intellectual or cognitive.

Each of the aspects of development will progress at slightly different rates for each individual during the various life stages, although broadly the picture is the same for most of us. Each life stage has its own characteristics in terms of the development. The **life stages** are:

- infancy – 0–1 year
- toddler – 1–2 years
- pre-school – 2–5 years

- childhood – 5–12 years
- adolescence – 12–18 years
- young adult – 18–40 years
- middle age – 40–65 years
- older age – over 65 years

Looking at the chart below will give you a broad understanding of the likely developmental stage any service user is in.

Developmental stages and chronological age

	Intellectual	Social/emotional	Language	Physical
Infant: Birth–1 year	Learns about things by feeling with hands and mouth	Attaches to parent(s), begins to recognise faces and smile; at about 6 months begins to recognise parent(s) and expresses fear of strangers; plays simple interactive games like peekaboo	Vocalises, squeals and imitates sounds; says simple words such as 'dada' and 'mama'	Lifts head first then chest; rolls over; pulls to sit; crawls and stands alone. Reaches for objects and takes up small items; grasps rattle

	Intellectual	Social/emotional	Language	Physical
Toddler: 1–2 years	Learns words for objects and people	Learns that self and parent(s) are different or separate from each other; imitates and performs tasks; indicates needs or wants without crying	Says some more complex words than 'dada' and 'mama'; follows simple instructions	Walks well; kicks; stoops and jumps in place; throws balls. Unbuttons clothes; builds tower of 4 cubes; scribbles; uses spoon; picks up very small objects
Pre-school: 2–5 years	Understands concepts such as tired, hungry and cold; recognises colours; becomes aware of numbers and letters	Begins to separate easily from parent(s); dresses with assistance; washes and dries hands; plays interactive games like tag	Names pictures; follows directions; can make simple sentences of two or three words; vocabulary increases	Runs well; hops; pedals tricycle; balances on one foot. Buttons clothes; builds tower of 8 cubes; copies simple figures or letters
School age: 5–12 years	Develops an understanding of numeracy and literacy concepts; learns relationship between objects and feelings; acquires knowledge and understanding	Acts independently, but is emotionally close to parent(s); dresses without assistance; joins same sex play groups and clubs	Defines words; knows and describes what things are made of; vocabulary increases	Skips; balances on one foot for 10 seconds; overestimates physical abilities. Draws person with 6 parts; copies detailed figures and objects
Adolescent: 12–18 years	Understands abstract concepts like illness and death; develops understanding of complex ideas	Experiences rapidly changing moods and behaviour; interested in peer group almost exclusively; distances from parent(s) emotionally; concerned with body image; likely to have first sexual relationship	Uses increased vocabulary; understands more abstract concepts like grief	May appear awkward and clumsy while learning to deal with rapid increases in size due to growth spurts

	Intellectual	Social/emotional	Language	Physical
Young adult: 18–40 years	Fully developed; continues to develop knowledge base related to education and/or job	Becomes independent from parent(s); develops own lifestyle and career; experiences social and economic changes; develops interests; chooses a partner; becomes a parent	Fully developed	Fully developed
Middle age: 40–65 years	Fully developed	Builds social and economic status; is fulfilled by work and/or family; children grow and leave nest; deals with ageing parents; copes with death of parents	Fully developed	Begins to experience physical changes of ageing: changing hair colour, lack of elasticity in skin, women experience menopause, reduction in muscular flexibility
Older adult: 65+ years	Fully developed	Adjusts to retirement; adjusts to loss of friends and relatives; copes with loss of spouse; adjusts to new role in family; copes with dying	Fully developed	Experiences more significant physical changes associated with ageing

Experience of development

The ways in which people have developed, and the influences on their development, will affect the services they now need and the ways in which these should be provided so that best use can be made of them.

Any major event which disrupts the expected pattern of development at any life stage will have a knock-on effect on future development.

For example, a child whose physical development is delayed at the toddler stage because of an accident will take a longer time than other children to learn to develop the co-ordination for throwing and catching, doing up buttons and placing objects on top of each other.

Provided that the accident did not cause any permanent damage, the child is likely to catch up and there is unlikely to be any significant difference in development by the time the child goes to school. However, an adolescent who experiences a major disruption to emotional development, such as the death of a parent or a traumatic divorce, may never recover from the interruption to the emotional development which should be taking place at that stage. All stages of development can be subject to interruption or delay, and this will affect the future development of the individual.

Sometimes development is delayed because of an illness, injury or disability which will have a long-term effect. A person who has cerebral palsy, for instance, will not follow a standard pattern of physical development. This does not mean that other aspects of his or her development will necessarily be impaired in any way. Someone who experiences a stroke in middle age may find that this interrupts the expected stage of social and emotional development which is usual for this life stage.

When considering the factors which impact on the service user, always consider the life events which are likely to have had an effect on their growth and development.

Check your learning

Think of each life stage you have passed through. Look at people older than yourself and consider the stages you have still to encounter.

Social history

It is not only personal history which has an impact on service users. The way in which society views people has an obvious effect on how they view themselves.

For example, most Western cultures have little regard for the contribution of older people. They are generally viewed as a group who need to be cared for and looked after, but do not have a contribution to make. Society makes provision for its older members by supplying health and care services, but it does not include them in plans for economic growth or for education. The wisdom and experience of older members of society is not generally valued. Unfortunately, this view that older members of society can no longer make a useful contribution can result in disrespectful and sometimes dangerous attitudes. Older people can be labelled 'wrinklies' or 'crumblies', and be regarded as a burden on society. This attitude does tend to disappear as individuals who hold it grow older themselves!

By contrast, many other cultures such as those in China or India have a great regard for older people, who are viewed as a source of wisdom and experience.

People with disabilities have often been regarded by society as needing to be cared for, and historically their independence has not been encouraged. It is only recently that, mainly due to the efforts of disabled people themselves, it has become understood that it is society and their environment which make life difficult for disabled people, and that any disability can be overcome if the right adaptations are made to their surroundings. The attitudes that have prevented disabled people from fully participating in society have resulted in disabled people finding it difficult to get work – some employers view them as not being capable and are unwilling to make the necessary changes to the work environment. This attitude has also contributed to many disabled people feeling that they are unable to undertake tasks for themselves, and that they need to depend on others for their care. It is easy to see how an unnecessary dependence on others and a lack of confidence can develop in many disabled people.

The way in which society regards groups of service users has influenced the ways services have been provided in the past, and still has an effect today. For example, the focus in care of older people is still quite strongly on residential care, and this is only slowly changing towards making use of the latest technology in order to provide innovative services such as telecare, which allow people to remain in the community and in their own homes.

Services for people with learning difficulties have only recently become more focused on allowing service users to live and participate in local communities, rather than providing care in a hospital-like environment.

The most noticeable effect of society's historical attitude to social care services is the question of empowerment. Services are still under the control of the service providers. It is still the organisations – regardless of the sector they belong to – which decide the type, quality and quantity of services provided. Even though service users are consulted and involved in the process, they do not make decisions.

This is slowly changing as the **direct payment system** extends. Direct payments are made by Social Services departments to the individuals concerned, who then become responsible for contracting and managing their own service provision. This approach is being used by many local authorities throughout the country – its use is being encouraged and is on the increase. Where direct payments are made, the individuals may choose services for which the local Social Services department or Health Authority already has arrangements, but if they wish they can advertise, recruit and employ their own carers and establish their own package of care.

Activity 5.2.1 Society's views of service user groups

During the period of a week, check newspapers and TV news items for mentions of the service user group you work with. Note down ways in which the attitudes of society are expressed. For example, are there any stories about older people achieving success, or are all the stories about how vulnerable older people are? Do the stories about disabled people have a patronising attitude?

Make notes about how the kinds of services you provide might have been influenced by these attitudes.

Responding to particular needs

Every service user has individual needs but, depending on the service user group you work with, you will need to learn about particular ways in which you can provide support.

For example, if you are working with young people with social and communication disorders such as autism, you will need to be trained to use particular communication skills which will help to reduce the differences between your methods of communication and theirs.

If you work with a service user group with sensory impairment such as hearing loss, you may need to learn how to sign or to lipspeak in order to reduce communication differences.

Service users who have little mobility will need you to learn how to move them comfortably and how to reduce the effects of remaining in one place for long periods of time.

Service users who have restricted use of hands and arms, or who have serious visual impairment, may need you to provide equipment which makes it possible for them to eat and drink.

(a)

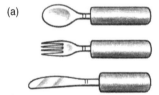

Light, thick-handled cutlery – people with arthritic hands will find these easy to hold

(e)

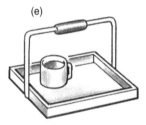

A person who is frail, or who only has the use of one arm, will find it possible to carry several items at once on a non-slip tray with a handle

(b)

An alternative to the feeding cup is to improvise with a glass with an angled straw or a teapot (not a metal one)

(f)

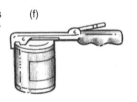

Specially-designed gadgets exist to help with taking the lids off jars

(c)

A feeding cup – remember that the liquid at the bottom is drunk first, so no tea leaves!

(g)

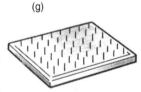

Someone who only has the use of one hand will be able to butter bread or peel potatoes using a spiked board

(d)

A person with the use of only one arm may find a deep bowl or a plate guard useful, especially when they are used with a combined knife and fork or a pusher spoon

All of the aids shown above are designed to allow people to maintain independence with only minimal assistance from others.

There are also special ways of helping people who have particular needs. For example, a visually impaired person is often able to feed himself or herself if you can help to prepare the plate of food in advance. If you arrange the food in separate portions around the plate and then tell the person, using a clockface as a comparison, that potatoes are at 2 o'clock, meat at 6 o'clock, sprouts at 8 o'clock, and so on, then this is often enough to allow the person to work out what he or she is eating and to enjoy the meal.

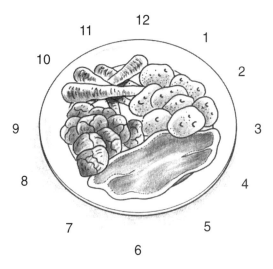

Care plans

Every service user will have a plan for his or her care. This will have been developed through discussion and consultation with the service user and those responsible for the care. The care plan will vary according to the work setting, but will include details of:

- the type of care to be provided
- details of any specific requirements, such as medications
- the ways in which care should be provided, with details such as times, and so on
- any particular requirements of the service user, such as diet
- information about moving and handling needs
- important social contacts for the service user
- contact details for relatives.

Every workplace will have its own style of care plan and you will need to be shown how to use the ones in your workplace correctly.

Following a care plan is essential. This makes it possible to be sure that the service user receives the same level of care from all of those involved in providing it. Professional carers do not work 24 hours a day (it just feels that way!) and they do have days off and holidays, so it is important that care services are provided by a team who all work in the same way. The care plan is the document that makes sure this happens, and that the team all work together. If a football team all played to slightly different rules, there would be chaos and a bad result! The same is true of care provision – all the team members should be delivering care to the same standard and in the same way. Following the care plan is the way to make sure this happens.

Responding to changing needs

Finally, remember that everyone changes and responds to events in their lives. Just because a service user has been assessed as needing a particular level and type of service at one point does not mean that this will continue indefinitely. The process of reviewing the services provided and checking that they are still appropriate and still meeting requirements is extremely important.

Many different events and influences can alter the needs that people have. All care plans have a regular review built in, which can be six-monthly or annual, and this is the time when service users and care workers have the opportunity to consider whether the service still meets the user's needs or if changes and adaptations need to be made.

People change and adapt throughout their lives, and many factors can bring about change. It is important that you are aware of changing needs and remain alert to the ways you may need to adapt the service to meet those needs.

Appendix: Links to the Induction Standards

Foundation Standards	Relevant Induction Standards	Link
1: Understand how to apply the value base of care 1.1 Promote empowerment of service users	1.1 The values 2.3 Role of the worker	The values you learned about in the Induction Standards are looked at in more depth in this Foundation Standard. You will consider how service users will benefit if you work in accordance with the values, and how you can work in an anti-discriminatory way. Your understanding of the ways service settings operate will help you to look at the issues raised for your own work.
1.2 Promote achievement and fulfilment	1.1 The values	
1.3 Recognise and work with constraints and conflicts	1.2 Worker relationships 5.1 The effect of the service setting on the service user 5.2 The effect of the service setting on the worker	
1.4 Promote anti-discriminatory practice	1.1 The values 1.2 Worker relationships	
2: Communicate effectively 2.1 Encourage communication	1.3 Communication	Everything you learned in the Induction Standards about verbal and non-verbal communication is important again here. This Foundation Standard looks more closely at the different aspects of communication and the way in which good communication helps you in your work. Also, a knowledge of policies and procedures, and an understanding of the importance of your role in maintaining confidentiality, will help you learn to keep good records.
2.2 Listen effectively	1.3 Communication	
2.3 Use physical contact effectively	1.3 Communication	
2.4 Promote communication where there are barriers and challenges	1.3 Communication	
2.5 Understand the principles of good record keeping	1.4 Confidentiality 2.1 Access to policies and procedures 2.2 Application of policies and procedures 2.3 Role of the worker	

Foundation Standards	Relevant Induction Standards	Link
3: Develop as a worker 3.1 Worker development	2.3 Role of the worker 5.2 The effect of the service setting on the worker	Some further aspects of your role and the ways in which you should relate to colleagues and supervisors are expanded in this Foundation Standard. You will also build on your knowledge about health and safety for service users by looking at your own health and safety at work.
3.2 Keeping safe and healthy	2.1 Access to policies and procedures 4.1 Moving and handling 4.2 Health and safety 4.3 Fire safety 4.4 Emergency first aid 4.5 Safe food handling 4.6 Infection control 5.2 The effect of the service setting on the worker	
4: Recognise and respond to abuse and neglect 4.1 Understand the nature of abuse	1.1 The values	The Induction Standards prepared you for some of the skills you need to help you recognise and respond to abuse and neglect. This Foundation Standard deals directly with the issues around abuse and neglect, and gives you information about how you can protect service users, and work within the policies of your service setting.
4.2 Understand the nature of neglect	1.1 The values 3.2 The particular needs of service user groups	
4.3 Recognise the signs and symptoms of abuse	1.2 Worker relationships	
4.4 Recognise the signs and symptoms of neglect	1.2 Worker relationships	
4.5 Understand when and how to respond to abuse and neglect	1.2 Worker relationships 1.4 Confidentiality 2.2 Application of policies and procedures	

Foundation Standards	Relevant Induction Standards	Link
5: Understand the experiences and particular needs of the individuals using the service 5.1 The nature of person/child-centred services	1.1 The values 1.2 Worker relationships 2.3 Role of the worker 3.1 The nature of the service user groups	In the Induction Standards you looked at the needs of groups of service users and how they were affected by the service setting. This Foundation Standard takes you to the next stage and encourages you to think about individuals' needs. You will consider how services can meet the particular needs of individuals, not just the general needs of groups.
5.2 The needs of the individuals within a person/child-centred service	3.2 The particular needs of service user groups 5.1 The effect of the service setting on the service user	

Useful websites

Care and Health magazine www.careandhealth.com

Care Homes for Older People: National Minimum Standards www.doh.gov.uk/ncsc

Care Standards Act (HMSO) http://www.hmso.gov.uk/acts/acts2000/20000014.htm

Department of Health www.doh.gov.uk

Health Development Agency www.hda-online.org.uk

Information Commissioner (Data Protection) www.dataprotection.gov.uk/

Investors in People www.iipuk.co.uk

National Care Homes Association www.ncha.gb.com

National Care Standards Commission www.carestandards.org.uk

NHS www.nhs.uk

Nursing and Midwifery Council www.nmc-uk.org

Social Care Association www.socialcareassoc.com

TOPSS - www.topss.org.uk

World Health Organization www.who.int

How the activities link to the outcomes of the Foundation Standards

Foundation Standard	Activity page
1.1.1 Understand what 'empowerment' means and why it is important to empower service users 1.1.2 Understand what a worker can do to empower the people they support	14
1.2.1 Enable the service users to develop or maintain a sense of achievement and fulfilment	18
1.3.1 Recognise and work with the constraints and conflicts created by living with others	19
1.3.2 Recognise and work with the constraint and conflicts created by working with others	21
1.4.1 Understand the terms: stereotyping, labelling, discrimination, anti-discrimination, oppression, anti-oppression 1.4.2 Understand how to behave in an anti-discriminatory way in the workplace and why this is important	24
2.1.1 Know factors that motivate people to communicate	28
2.2.1 Know how communication can be promoted through effective listening 2.2.2 Demonstrate effective listening skills	35
2.3.1 Understand how to use physical contact to promote communication 2.3.2 Understand when the use of physical contact is inappropriate	38
2.5.1 Know the use and purpose of each record or report the worker has to use or contribute to 2.5.3 Understand the issues of confidentiality in relation to each record or report the worker uses or contributes to	47
2.5.2 Demonstrate the ability to make written records that are: legible and readable; relevant to purpose; clear and concise; factual and checkable 2.5.4 Understand issues of accountability relating to record keeping	48

Foundation Standard	Activity page
3.1.2 Demonstrate appropriate preparation, participation and follow up in relation to training/development opportunities	56
3.1.3 Demonstrate effective use of supervision	58
3.2.2 Know the importance of maintaining a good diet and taking appropriate rest and relaxation when not at work	68
3.2.3 Recognise the symptoms of stress and know what action to take in the event of this	71
4.1.1 Understand the following different forms of abuse: physical, sexual, emotional, financial, institutional	77
4.3.1 Recognise the possible signs/symptoms associated with the following forms of abuse: physical, sexual, emotional, financial, institutional	84
4.5.1 Demonstrate when to report abuse/neglect 4.5.2 Demonstrate how to report and record abuse/neglect	89
5.1.1 Understand the importance of seeing the service user as central to service provision 5.1.2 Understand the importance of a 'holistic approach' when planning/providing services	97
5.1.3 Understand the possible tensions between the needs/wishes of service users and the ability of the organisation to provide for them	100
5.2.1 Understand the impact of history on the individual receiving the service	107

Matching Grid for the TOPSS Induction and Foundation Standards

Foundation Standards	Relevant Induction Standards	Link
1: Understand how to apply the value base of care 1.1 Promote empowerment of service users	 1.1 The values 2.3 Role of the worker	Develops the values introduced in the induction standards to promote empowerment and a feeling of achievement and fulfilment for service users. It also further develops an understanding of anti-discriminatory practice.
1.2 Promote achievement and fulfilment	1.1 The values	The values you learned about in the Induction Standards are looked at in more depth in the Foundation Standards. You can see that working in accordance with the values means that service users will benefit. You should be able to see how the values you use mean that you can work in a way which is anti-discriminatory. Much of the understanding you have about how service settings operate will help you to look at the issues this raises for your work.
1.3 Recognise and work with constraints and conflicts	1.2 Worker relationships 5.1 The effect of the service setting on the service user 5.2 The effect of the service setting on the worker	
1.4 Promote anti-discriminatory practice	1.1 The values 1.2 Worker relationships	
2: Communicate effectively 2.1 Encourage communication	 1.3 Communication	Develops aspects of communication and confidentiality. Also relates to applying the policies and procedures essential for the worker to carry out his or her role effectively.
2.2 Listen effectively	1.3 Communication	Everything you looked at in the Induction Standards about verbal and non-verbal communication is important again here. Foundation Standards look more closely at the different aspects of communication and the way in which good communication helps you in your work.
2.3 Use physical contact effectively	1.3 Communication	
2.4 Promote communication where there are barriers and challenges	1.3 Communication 1.4 Confidentiality 2.1 Access to policies and procedures 2.2 Using policies and procedures 2.3 The role of the worker	

Foundation Standards	Relevant Induction Standards	Link
2.5 Understand the principles of good record keeping		Policies and procedures, as well as an understanding of the importance of your role in maintaining confidentiality, are essential in being able to keep good records
3: Develop as a worker 3.1 Worker development	2.3 Role of the worker 5.2 The effect of the service setting on the worker	Develops understanding of the effects of the service setting on service provision, and of maintaining safety.
3.2 Keeping safe and healthy	2.1 Access to policies and procedures 4.1. Moving and handling 4.2. Health and safety 4.3 Fire safety 4.4 Emergency first aid 4.5 Safe food handling 4.6 Infection control 5.2 The effect of the service setting on the worker	Some of the aspects of your role and the ways in which you relate to colleagues and supervisors are expanded in this Foundation Standard. You also build on your knowledge about health and safety for service users by looking at your own health and safety at work.
4: Recognise and respond to abuse and neglect 4.1 Understand the nature of abuse	1.1 The values	Builds on the basic understanding of abuse and neglect, and further equips workers with the knowledge and skills necessary to contribute to the protection of service users from abuse.
4.2 Understand the nature of neglect	1.1 The values 3.2 The particular needs of service user groups	The Induction standards will have prepared you for some of the skills you need to help you to recognise and respond to abuse and neglect. The Foundation Standard deals directly with the issues around abuse and neglect and gives you information about how you can protect service users, and work within the policies of your service setting
4.3 Recognise the signs and symptoms of abuse	1.2 Worker relationships	
4.4 Recognise the signs and symptoms of neglect	1.2 Worker relationships	
4.5 Understand when and how to respond to abuse and neglect	1.2 Worker relationships 1.4 Confidentiality 2.2 Application of policies and procedures	

Foundation Standards	Relevant Induction Standards	Link
5: Understand the experiences and particular needs of the individuals using the service 5.1 The nature of person/child-centred services	1.1 The values 1.2 Worker relationships 2.3 Role of the worker 3.1 The nature of the service user groups	Builds on understanding of the experiences and needs of the service user groups, and attempts to enable the worker to move from considering the broad experiences and needs of a group to seeing the individual service user in the context of that group. Introduces the concept of care planning from a perspective that is person/child-centred and takes individual history and experience as the starting point.
5.2 The needs of the individuals within a person/child-centred service	3.2 The particular needs of service user groups 5.1 The effect of the service setting on the service user	In the Induction standards you looked at the needs of groups of service users and how they were affected by the service setting. The Foundation standard takes this to the next stage and encourages you to think about individuals and the needs they have. You will need to think about how services can meet the needs of individuals, not just the general needs of particular groups.

Other titles of interest

The best-selling book for success in S/NVQ Level 2 in Care
0435 45224 X

TEL: 01865 888080
FAX: 01865 314029

E-MAIL: orders@heinemann.co.uk
WEB: www.heinemann.co.uk

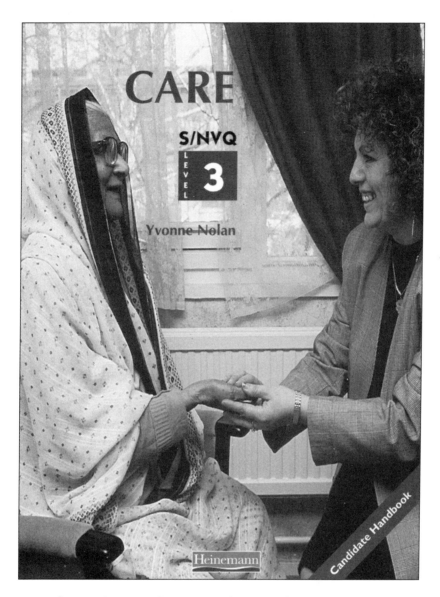

A complete and concise learning package for the S/NVQ Level 3 in Care
0435 45642 3

TEL: 01865 888080   E-MAIL: orders@heinemann.co.uk
FAX: 01865 314029   WEB: www.heinemann.co.uk